# Cambridge Elements

Elements in Politics and Society in Southeast Asia
edited by
Edward Aspinall
*Australian National University*
Meredith L. Weiss
*University at Albany, SUNY*

# INDONESIA

## Twenty Years of Democracy

Jamie S. Davidson
*National University of Singapore*

CAMBRIDGE
UNIVERSITY PRESS

## CAMBRIDGE
### UNIVERSITY PRESS

University Printing House, Cambridge CB2 8BS, United Kingdom

One Liberty Plaza, 20th Floor, New York, NY 10006, USA

477 Williamstown Road, Port Melbourne, VIC 3207, Australia

314–321, 3rd Floor, Plot 3, Splendor Forum, Jasola District Centre,
New Delhi – 110025, India

79 Anson Road, #06–04/06, Singapore 079906

Cambridge University Press is part of the University of Cambridge.

It furthers the University's mission by disseminating knowledge in the pursuit of
education, learning, and research at the highest international levels of excellence.

www.cambridge.org
Information on this title: www.cambridge.org/9781108459082
DOI: 10.1017/9781108686518

© Jamie S. Davidson 2018

First published 2018

*A catalogue record for this publication is available from the British Library.*

ISBN 978-1-108-45908-2 Paperback
ISSN 2515-2998 (online)
ISSN 2515-298X (print)

# Indonesia

## Twenty Years of Democracy

Politics and Society in Southeast Asia

DOI: 10.1017/9781108686518
First published online: August 2018

Jamie S. Davidson
*National University of Singapore*

**Abstract:** This Element argues that after twenty years of democratization, Indonesia has performed admirably. This is especially so when the country's accomplishments are placed in comparative perspective. However, as we analytically focus more closely to inspect Indonesia's political regime, political economy, and how identity-based mobilizations have emerged, it is clear that Indonesia still has many challenges to overcome, some so pressing that they could potentially erode or reverse many of the democratic gains the country has made since its former authoritarian ruler, Soeharto, was forced to resign in 1998.

**Keywords:** Indonesian politics, political economy, identity-based mobilizations, democratization

ISBNs: 9781108459082 (PB) 9781108686518 (OC)
ISSNs: 2515-2998 (online) 2515-298X (print)

# Contents

# 1 Introduction

On May 21, 1998, Indonesian president Soeharto shocked the country when he announced his resignation, after some thirty-two years of authoritarian rule, in a brief televised speech. Following constitutional procedure, the former army general immediately transferred power to B. J. Habibie, a civilian, whom Soeharto had handpicked as vice president months earlier. Broadcast from the presidential palace in the nation's bustling capital of Jakarta to tens of millions viewers across the country and out into the world, Soeharto's resignation suddenly thrust Indonesia onto an arduous journey toward an unknown future. Democracy was one likely direction – certainly a desired direction for millions of Indonesians. To some surprise, slightly more than a year after Soeharto's resignation, Habibie oversaw the implementation of Indonesia's first national, democratic elections since 1955. Few predicted then what is hardly disputable today: that Indonesia would become Southeast Asia's freest democracy for the better part of two decades.

Shortly after leading a massacre of a half-million or more members and supporters (both real and suspected) of the powerful Communist Party of Indonesia in 1965 and 1966, Soeharto became president (Roosa 2006; Kammen & McGregor 2012; Robinson 2018; Melvin 2018[1]). During his long tenure, he survived a number of challenges to his authority. By 1998, however, the combined successive pressures of a regional economic collapse, student protests, urban middle-class dissatisfaction, elite defection, urban riots, and a polarized military overwhelmed the septuagenarian leader. The post–Cold War context also affected his staying power. With the disappearance of the international Communist "threat" from the early 1990s on, the United States had far less need to support local, rightwing strongmen. Instead, it was inclined to promote freedom and free trade, encouraging the removal of other countries' (not its own) domestic protectionist barriers and allowing US companies wider access to foreign markets. Indonesia, with its 200-million-plus population, was a prime market.[2] Under Soeharto's regime, capitalists, including foreign ones, had long thrived. But the former general also promoted and protected companies belonging to friends and family members. Although the economy grew, as these companies transformed into conglomerates they began to crowd out foreign investment in lucrative sectors. Corruption also ran rampant. With Soeharto at the helm, neither

---

[1] See also Joshua Oppenheimer's two compellingly controversial films, *The Act of Killing* (2012) and *The Look of Silence* (2014).

[2] Today Indonesia's population has topped 260 million and is expected to surpass the 300 million mark by 2035, which will make it the world's third most populous country.

Indonesia's economy nor its government would ever be as open as the United States now wanted. All told, given the regime's domination of the country's politics, economy, and society, for Indonesians Soeharto's political demise meant fundamental changes would ensue. In 1998, however, the extent of these changes, and whether they would be for good or ill, were anyone's guess. The period was marked by palpable uncertainty.

It has now been two decades since Soeharto left office and democracy replaced dictatorship. Elsewhere scholars have deemed twenty to twenty-five years an appropriate point in time to look back and assess the many facets of regime change (Hanson 2017). This Element will explore how Indonesia has changed, and how it has not. Employing what I hope is a productive framework, I advance three principal arguments.

The first argument suggests that Indonesian democratization looks strong in comparative perspective, but that it looks much weaker when viewed up close. As of 2018, post-Soeharto Indonesia has held four national parliamentary elections, three direct presidential elections, and more than 1,000 local elections. Democracy across this sprawling 17,000-island nation has shown resilience. The rotation of elites through office has been largely peaceful, and most Indonesians view the electoral process as fair and legitimate. Remarkably few citizens have been killed in direct connection to elections as they (especially journalists) have in the older democracy of the Philippines. There also has been nothing comparable to the extrajudicial killings of civilians by state agents – as many as 13,000, according to human rights groups – that President Rodrigo Duterte has encouraged with his war against drugs. Disproportionately, this spree of state violence has targeted the urban poor.

Indonesia's press is relatively free, and none of the post-Soeharto presidents has been embroiled in corruption scandals like that in nearby Malaysia, where former prime minister Najib Razak has been accused of misappropriating more than US$700 million in state-related funds. Electoral manipulation there in favor of the ruling United Malays National Organization has been rampant, with severe gerrymandering a favored ploy. The manipulation helped this party and its electoral allies maintain parliamentary control from the 1950s, when elections were first instituted, until 2018, when the opposition won a stunning electoral victory. In neighboring Singapore the domineering People's Action Party has used similar tactics to win elections uninterruptedly. Meanwhile, Vietnam does not even hold national-level elections; it remains a one-party authoritarian state. And in Thailand, the military, unlike its Indonesian counterpart, continues to stage coups whenever it perceives political stalemates as insurmountable. The military staged its latest coups in 2006 and 2014, and has applied draconian laws to stifle dissent. This includes the extensive execution of the kingdom's infamous *lèse majesté* laws and the insertion of a provision (Article 44) in the temporary constitution that gives today's ruling junta near absolute powers.

To Thailand's west, Myanmar's military, in power since 1962, took the world by surprise when it initiated a transition toward democracy in the isolationist country. Here, however, political liberalization has helped to ignite a virulent form of Buddhist nationalism that has resulted in the murder of thousands of Muslim Rohingyas and the forcible displacement of hundreds of thousands more from their home province in the country's west. Refugees have recounted horrifying atrocities. Farther afield, Turkey (and Indonesia) had been celebrated as a model of Muslim democracy – until its Islamist president, Recep Tayyip Erdogan, made a power grab as a result of a failed military coup in mid-2016. More than eighteen months later, the country remains in a state of emergency, and Erdogan's regime has arrested some 50,000 opponents. Post-Soeharto Indonesia also has not experienced the sharp reversals (at least not yet) that have plunged countries of the Arab Spring (except Tunisia) back into harsh authoritarianism. Indonesia's democracy, however flawed, has also outlasted efforts of institutionalizing open politics in another vast, multiethnic polity with a marked despotic past: Russia. Who said making democracy work was easy?

The counterpoint to these observations, however, is that by shifting one's gaze from this broad comparative perspective to a county-specific vantage point, some of the luster on Indonesia's democracy is lost. State institutions, weakened by decades of overbearing interference and a crippling politicization, are compromised and corruptible; this is especially so for those institutions tasked with upholding the rule of law. Inequality is on the rise, poverty alleviation too slow, and the creation of jobs in the formal sector slower still. "Money politics" infects elections and legislation-making at all government levels. While the country's multiparty system has proven more robust than that of the Philippines or Thailand, the system is cracking under the weight of corruption and the rise of vote-buying. Although much of the ethno-religious and separatist bloodshed that marred Indonesia's transition to democracy has thankfully waned, everyday security remains uncertain for too many Indonesians. Decentralization, designed to empower local communities, has contributed to the country's continuing corruption and to many incidents of collective violence. Local elites have built their power by skimming off government transfers instead of by improving service delivery and development outcomes. Growing sectarianism threatens civility and civil rights, especially of minorities. And although the military no longer determines policy on most civilian matters, its informal power rightly worries advocates of civilian democracy.

These deficits might give pause to classifying Indonesia as a democracy, but not for this author. My second argument contends that democracy, and its related process of democratization, is the most appropriate overarching framework for studying Indonesia, as this Element does in examining complex, interlocking developments in post-Soeharto Indonesia across political, economic, and societal realms. Changes in each of these aspects condition changes in the others. Most observers do concur that the country is a democracy. But glancing over a list of modifying adjectives offered by these scholars indicates what they think of the quality of this democracy: young, defective, electoral, weak, illiberal, procedural, patronage, or patrimonial.

By insisting that Indonesia is a democracy, however wobbly, I do not mean to stifle debate – quite the opposite. Democracy is notoriously difficult to pin down and define appropriately. Rightly or wrongly, it means different things to different people. Even among scholars there is no consensus over democracy's definition. My central focus is on tensions, inconsistencies, and contradictory puzzles of Indonesia's democracy. I could have chosen to explore Indonesia through a different lens: globalization versus nationalism, corruption versus good governance, sectarianism versus secularism, economic growth versus equitable development, oligarchy versus pluralism, or decentralization versus recentralization. But each of these dueling themes will be addressed in relation to the successes and deficits of Indonesia's democracy throughout this Element.

Using the workings and failings of Indonesia's democratic order as my analytical schema, I do not mean to imply that Indonesia's democracy is consolidated, or "the only game in town" (a popular saying among political scientists). Fixating on consolidation closes debate, foregrounds static outcomes, and ignores the dynamic processes of and challenges to democracy in current Indonesia. Today, nowhere is democracy safe. It is always threatened with rollback or attenuation, and its quality everywhere is always open for improvement. Indonesia is no exception.

Making democracy the central focus – but conceived as an unfinished process replete with conflicts over power, resources, ideas, and institutions – also allows us to consider how the impact of regime change twenty years on has affected the dizzying diversity of Indonesians across the vast archipelago. Indonesia is a "super diverse" country (Goebel 2015). Its islands stretch across a distance slightly greater than New York to Los Angeles; those islands are home to some 300 ethnic groups, who together speak more than 700 languages, eighteen of which are classified as institutionalized.[3] Any analysis of politics, economy, and society must account for the unevenness of democracy's impact and quality within Indonesia and the immense variation in the ways people experience it in everyday life. Democracy has been a boon for some, a bane for others. Many of its outcomes have been unanticipated or unintended (if not, in some cases, unwanted).

My third argument moves beyond the primary comparative project of assessing whether today's Indonesia has or has not changed from the Soeharto (or New Order) period. A "change and continuities" framework has dominated post-Soeharto Indonesian studies. Scholars identify or show how specific legacies of three decades of dictatorship have survived the transition or, conversely, demonstrate how emergent developments and dynamics have since overwhelmed or buried such legacies. A typical answer often is that there has been "a bit of both" – hence the approach's other moniker: "changing continuities." But, to my mind, after two decades of fruitful findings, this analytical exercise has run its course. Twenty years after Soeharto gives us ample time, context, and evidence to establish discrete temporal periods *within* democratic Indonesia.

The changing continuities schema mistakenly conceives the New Order and post–New Order periods as monolithic, glossing over the deep changes that occurred within each historical era. For example, there is little appreciation of the evolution of methods and tactics Soeharto deployed to dominate the country for more than three decades. This framework commits a similar mistake in portraying the post–New Order era.

Scholars also have fixated on "changing continuities" more than in post-communist Eastern Europe or the post-Marcos Philippines, for example, because of the decades-long expansion of the economy under Soeharto. The economies of the Soviet bloc and the Philippines under Marcos stagnated or floundered. This contrast has given rise to a contested normative question over whether the New Order proved good or bad for Indonesia.

Differing interpretations of Indonesia's economic growth have divided the country's scholars. Those on the right believe that the political stability Soeharto imposed is responsible for the considerable economic expansion and for lifting millions from abject poverty. Scholars on the left insist the macroeconomic numbers did not change the lives of the masses as much as is claimed. Economic growth was in any case predicated on a culture of fear and violence, the killing of hundreds of thousands, the hollowing out of rule-of-law institutions, the enabling of a culture of corruption, and the rapacious degrading

---

[3]  Taken from the informative website ethnologue.com.

of the environment and the country's natural resources. These polarizing views persisted to the regime's very end.

A similar debate has spilled into the post-Soeharto period with contrasting understandings of the Asian Financial Crisis of 1997/98, which precipitated Soeharto's downfall. The right saw the financial crisis as an aberration and stressed that its origins were outside the country (in Bangkok, to be more precise). The crisis therefore was not the regime's doing, and was beyond its control. Achievements of the post-Soeharto period are then attributed to legacies of the Soeharto years – fiscal discipline and good economic growth, to name just two examples. Furthermore, the problems of today are products of the new democratic order, including a worsening investment climate caused largely by an unsteady policy environment and a chaotic diffusion of corruption enablers and opportunists. For left-leaning scholars, the financial crisis only exposed the true rot of the New Order regime. That it all began in Thailand and spread throughout Southeast Asia does not explain why the economic crisis in Indonesia was so profound and why it swiftly led to the downfall of a regime that appeared to be entrenched in every aspect of the life of Indonesians. Many of the challenges to Indonesia's democracy are thus Soeharto's legacies.

I make the case that the post-Soeharto era can be divided into three main periods, which correspond to the divisions of my sections in this Element. Each section is further divided into three subsections: a politics subsection scrutinizes party politics, electoral outcomes, changing rules of the electoral and party systems, and the local politics of decentralization; a political economy subsection examines contestation over how Indonesia's trillion-dollar economy is managed and by what means groups access state benefits and the country's trove of natural resources; a third subsection grapples with the rise of old and new identity-based mobilizations of marginalized groups and their impact on local society and national politics.

Section 2, Innovation, covers the transition from authoritarianism. It shows how the period's fluidity bred a myriad of reforms, some successful, others less so. The uncertainty of the transition – the uncertainty also of its direction – thrust millions back into economic despair on Java and contributed to separatist-related and communal bloodshed in the country's outer islands. But it was also a period of ferment and optimism – perhaps above all an optimism that a new democratic order was consonant with the country's complex social fabric.

Section 3, Stagnation, demonstrates how optimistic aspirations were dashed.[4] Indonesia's two-term president Susilo Bambang Yudhoyono (2004–9, 2009–14)

---

[4] Describing the Yudhoyono period as a time of stagnation was first used by Tomsa (2010).

was a victim of outsized expectations. Juggling the competing interests of an avaricious and unruly parliamentary coalition, but buoyed by strong economic growth thanks to a commodity boom, Yudhoyono slowed the pace of reform to a halt. Procedurally, Indonesia remained democratic, but Yudhoyono's governments failed to improve the quality of that democracy meaningfully. In fact, attacks against minorities indicated that some gains were being reversed.

Section 4, Polarization, details how a potentially destabilizing divide has emerged in the post-Yudhoyono period. Indonesia's current president, Joko "Jokowi" Widodo, is both cause and effect of the severing of political Islam and pluralism and their division into opposing camps. Of course, any dichotomy misses cross-cutting alliances and obscures rifts within each bloc. For example, leaders on both sides claim to be ardent nationalists.

While struggles over material resources in democratic Indonesia has been unceasing (if not debilitating), these sections explain the progression from contestation over the design and control of governance institutions to fierce politicking over state ideology, national identity, and citizenship. This conflict will amplify as Indonesia prepares for its fourth direct presidential election in 2019. The conclusion (Section 5) examines the sources of threats to Indonesia's hard-won democracy and suggests a research agenda to help better explain and understand the country's possible futures.

## 2 Innovation

This section charts Indonesia's early transition period (1998 to 2004), a time of uncertainty, ferment, hope, and despair. The country's institutional political and economic landscape underwent significant changes. Politicians, civil society activists, and other reformers sought to liberalize the country's political system – most concretely expressed in holding free and fair elections, amending the constitution, and decentralizing the country's governance framework. In response to economic collapse, the International Monetary Fund dictated the direction of reforms to open up the country's economy. As millions of Indonesians were thrust back into poverty, elements tied to the New Order regime ensured that resistance to political and economic liberalization remained stiff. Just how much regime change there was at this point was open to question – for example, the army was still a formidable actor, although its influence in the public sphere was on the wane.

Meanwhile, dynamic identity-based mobilizations accompanied the institutional innovations of this unstable and permissive period. In particular, three minorities which had suffered acutely under Soeharto's rule – conservative Muslims, ethnic Chinese, and outer-island indigenous peoples – made claims on resources and sought to elevate their status in society before the window of opportunity shut. Some of this contentiousness touched off horrific violence, although its extent varied considerably across the archipelago. In all, while Indonesia "was a laggard in the wave that saw procedural democracy restored across much of Latin America, the Soviet bloc and Sub-Saharan Africa by the mid-1990s, along with the toppling of dictators in the Philippines, Korea and Taiwan" (Kuddus 2017, 45), the country was now seeking to move away from decades of authoritarianism to join the world's club of democracies.

## 2.1 Politics

As a Soeharto protégé, President Habibie surprised observers by the steps he took to bring democracy back to Indonesia. During his brief tenure (May 1998 to October 1999), the German-trained engineer lifted press restrictions, released political prisoners, and oversaw the crafting of the rules for Indonesia's foundational legislative election of 1999. In this electoral contest, which received ample financial and technical support from the West, forty-eight parties participated (Anwar 2010). Only three had been permitted to run in the New Order's scripted ballots.

Subsequently, the selection of the president was made via a supreme parliament that, as an institution, had "chosen" Soeharto as president six times between 1967 and 1997.[5] Although the Indonesian Democratic Party of Struggle (Partai Demokrasi Indonesia-Perjuangan, PDI-P) topped the 1999 polls, with only one-third of the votes it would need allies to rule and to capture the presidency. The Islamic parties, led by Amien Rais of the National Mandate Party (Partai Amanat Nasional, PAN), conspired to deny Megawati Sukarnoputri, PDI-P's chairwoman, the presidency. Parliamentary deal-making resulted in the selection of Abdurrahman Wahid, also known as Gus Dur, a blind Muslim cleric from the Islamic National Awakening Party (Partai Kebangkitan Bangsa, PKB). Wahid had a reputation for unstinting commitment to religious pluralism. By any account or measure, the 1999 election was a triumph of democracy in a country known for being not democratic.

There were reforms elsewhere. The army, under pressure from civil society organizations regarding the human rights abuses its soldiers committed during the New Order, agreed to reduce the number of seats it held in the supreme parliament; by 2004, it removed its representation altogether. The military also renounced its doctrine of dual-function

---

[5]  It is known as the People's Consultative Council (Majelis Permusyawaratan Rakyat, MPR).

(*dwifungsi*) and its policy of seconding officers to civilian positions (*kekaryaan*), both of which had allowed it to play a pivotal role in the country's social and political affairs under Soeharto. Finally, the military released the police from institutional control. The now autonomous police was expected to take the lead in domestic security matters.

A series of constitutional amendments, debated and adopted by parliament from 1999 to 2002, led to further institutional innovations (King 2003; Horowitz 2013). Some amendments sought to guarantee Indonesians a range of freedoms and democratic rights that were lacking in the country's short 1945 constitution. Then there was the introduction of a five-year presidential term with a single second possible term. This mechanism was intended to prevent any political leader from bringing back dictatorship. In 2002, the third round of constitutional amendments introduced direct presidential elections.[6] Initially, President Megawati, who had been elevated from her vice-presidency position in 2001 after parliament impeached Gus Dur over corruption allegations, had opposed direct presidential elections.[7] Civil society organizations and most parties advocated the change. The former insisted that it empowered the people. The political parties felt leaving the presidential selection to parliament – whose powers had been enhanced to counteract the executive-heavy governance of Soeharto's New Order – had produced excessive uncertainty and division (Crouch 2010). Three presidents in less than two years was proof of that.

The same constitutional amendment process also established a Constitutional Court. Its subsequent implementing law gave it the power of judicial review – an authority that in theory runs counter to Indonesia's civil law tradition (Lev 2000).[8] One motive for establishing the court included the emasculation of the existing Supreme Court. Drowning in a vast backlog of cases, the Court still had not recovered from decades of institutional decay and overbearing political interference; it was incapable of taking on a new responsibility of impartially protecting the people's new constitutional rights and freedoms (Pompe 2005). Parliamentarians also desired to follow in the footsteps of other new democracies, including Thailand, South Africa, and South Korea, where constitutional courts had been established (Davidson 2009; Mietzner 2010). Since its founding, the court has forced the state to uphold its

---

[6] A weak and ineffectual upper chamber of parliament was also created, largely to placate regional aspirations.

[7] Wahid also had antagonized the army over involvement in key personnel decisions.

[8] The Constitutional Court was granted the power to hear cases concerning the constitutionality of laws and the authority of state bodies, the dissolution of political parties, electoral disputes, and impeachment. Its decisions are binding.

obligations to provide access to a fair trial, to protect its citizens from corruption, and to guarantee other rights. In accord with new human rights principles enshrined in the constitution, it lifted the ban on political participation by those associated, or those thought to be associated, with the banned Communist Party of Indonesia (Butt 2007).

If the Constitutional Court is conceived as a corrective to the New Order's disregard of the rule of law, then the 1999 constitutional amendment devolving significant administrative and fiscal powers to local government units was a similar measure addressing the coercive centralization of the New Order regime (Malley 1999). Historically, there was precedent for decentralizing authority to the regions (Booth 2011). The regions certainly desired it. Local elites salivated over the resources, which came in two main forms: block grants from the central government, and greater proportions of revenue generated from local resource extraction. But a supply-side argument also suggests that regional autonomy came to fruition because an Indonesian team of US-trained technocrats who designed its framework convinced Habibie of the political necessity to pass such legislation (Smith 2008). Decentralization was codified in two subsequent parliamentary statutes passed in 1999 (one on administration, the other on fiscal matters) and put into effect in 2001.

When this new regional autonomy began to take effect, it created new possibilities, but also concerns about the weakened powers of the Indonesian state (Aspinall & Fealy 2003; van Klinken & Barker 2009). Decentralization's promoters maintain that autonomous local governments improve development outcomes by bringing officialdom closer to the people and by increasing the efficiency of the provisions of local goods. Regional autonomy laws thus devolved responsibilities for health care, education, land use, spatial planning, and other powers to rural districts and urban municipalities.[9] More than two million national civil servants, mostly teachers, became regional civil servants. Decentralization is also supposed to bolster "good governance" by galvanizing local citizen participation, including that by nongovernmental organizations, which are expected to partner with local governments to find creative solutions to governance problems. On the other hand, decentralization, in theory, relieves the central government of the heavy financial burden of paying for such key welfare services as health and education, and favors technocratic, non- redistributive approaches to what are in fact political problems (Hadiz 2010). While decentralization placed matters pertaining to land

---

[9] The central government retained competency over foreign affairs, monetary and fiscal policy, religious affairs, defense and security, and the judiciary.

in local government hands, for instance, there was no insistence on land redistribution to society's neediest. These features help explain why skeptics attack decentralization as a pro-market, neoliberal Trojan Horse.

Decentralization initiated what is arguably democratic Indonesia's most unintended outcome – the proliferation or splitting up of provinces and districts. Under decades of New Order rule, the number of provinces held steady at twenty-seven. By 2012, the number had increased to thirty-four (even with the loss of the province of East Timor). Districts and municipalities grew from fewer than 250 during the New Order to more than 500 today. While many observers were transfixed by the country's external boundaries during the messy transition to democracy – fearing that Indonesia might break apart, akin to Yugoslavia and the Soviet Union (Estrade 1998; Rhode 2001) – the country's internal boundary lines underwent the more dramatic transformation (Bünte 2009; Kimura 2012).

Because revenue from natural-resource exploitation had largely flowed into central government coffers under Soeharto, the return of larger portions of these monies to their area of origin was fundamental to decentralization. The 1999 regional autonomy law on fiscal matters entitled local governments to receive 80 percent of the revenue from local forestry and mining, 30 percent from natural gas, and 15 percent from oil.[10] But central officials feared such largesse might create strong provinces with the means to challenge central government authority, or even spark new separatist demands, especially in such resource-rich provinces as East Kalimantan and Riau. To preclude that possibility, the decentralization laws made the smaller administrative unit of the district, and not the province, the autonomous level of government. Decentralization thus channeled unprecedented amounts of resources into district and city governments.

But for some regional elites, or aspiring challengers, decentralization's largesse was insufficient; not everyone was in position to reap the material rewards. Fearing exclusion, some aspirants hit upon an ingenious plan: demand one's own province or district. The success of such particularistic interest was possible because the splitting of regional governments was, in theory, in line with the discourse of bringing government closer to the people. Regional elites were not the only ones trying to benefit from decentralization; central officials in charge of approving a new government's application were themselves in a position to accept illegal payments (Schulte Nordholt 2003). Lastly, in some

---

[10] The law has since been amended more than once, but the basic percentages of distribution have remained unchanged. These amounts are further divided among the home district, the other districts in the province, and the provincial government.

cases, national party elites realized that counterparts in local party branches would benefit electorally from the split (Pierskalla 2016).

### 2.1.1 Contra Innovation

Institutional innovation, however, did not lead to an inexorable deepening of Indonesia's democracy. Countervailing forces abounded. The situation was in flux; just how much real change was happening was unclear. Consider the results of the celebrated 1999 elections. Parties associated with the New Order – the nationalist secular PDI-P, the Islamic United Development Party (Partai Persatuan Pembangunan, PPP[11]), and the New Order regime's electoral vehicle, Golkar – obtained 67 percent of the votes and about 72 percent of parliamentary seats. If we add the two Islamic parties associated with Indonesia's old, established Muslim social organizations (PAN with Muhammadiyah and PKB with Nahdlatul Ulama[12]), the numbers gained by parties with ties to the old New Order became approximately 86 percent and 90 percent, respectively. The strong showing of these parties, especially the controversial survival of Soeharto's Golkar, coupled with the evisceration under the New Order of independent labor unions and peasant associations, reflected the fact that much of the New Order's ruling class remained politically active.[13] Ultimately, this outcome ensured the circumscribed, conservative outcome of the transition (Robison & Hadiz 2004; Lane 2008). This development was graphically illustrated by the tendency of the establishment parties to work together to ensure that each party shared in the spoils of lucrative ministry appointments (Slater 2004). This collusion minimized the accountability of elected representatives to their constituencies. Viewed from this perspective, we see how the parties' motives for introducing direct presidential elections, as was mentioned earlier, were not entirely selfless. Leaders of the main parties succeeded in monopolizing the electoral process by forbidding independent avenues to candidature.

Security-sector reforms were circumscribed too. First, the military defended its self- and off-budget financing.[14] Each branch of the armed forces and many units within each branch own large foundations, hotels, shopping malls, and

---

[11] At this point, "Islamic" is an apt description; over the course of the democratic era, it became more "Islamist."

[12] Muhammadiyah was established in 1912, Nahdlatul Ulama in 1926.

[13] Some considered Golkar's survival a blessing in disguise. Horowitz (2013) argues forcefully that Golkar's agreement to the electoral and constitutional reforms acted as a stabilizing force in a time of great uncertainty and that Golkar's participation in the negotiated, methodical transition lent the process the necessary legitimacy and buy-in from elites.

[14] Off-budget accounting is prevalent among most (if not all) ministries (MacIntyre 2000; Baker 2015).

tracts of land, and are engaged in a host of other semilegal and illegal enterprises, all of which has been justified as filling budgetary gaps. Second, the military stymied reform of its territorial command structure. Under the New Order, this hierarchical structure bolstered tight societal control by creating parallel military units alongside local civilian governments across the archipelago. To be expected, the military's territorial command structure and its self-financing practices have been mutually reinforcing.

Lastly, the transition's uncertainty helped to spark bloodshed around the country's extensive periphery. Following East Timor's 1999 independence referendum, the armed forces, angered by President Habibie's decision to offer the vote in the first place, and pro-integration local militias conducted a scorched-earth campaign. Hundreds of East Timorese died, and hundreds of thousands were forced by the military across the border into West Timor (Tanter, Ball, & van Klinken 2006; Robinson 2009).

East Timor's exit from Indonesia encouraged the independence movement in Aceh, some 5,000 kilometers to the west. As Acehnese civil-society organizations began mobilizing large pro-independence demonstrations, the Indonesian army stepped up its operations against the movement's existing armed secessionist wing, the Free Aceh Movement (Gerakan Aceh Merdeka), which had been waging a low-intensity rebellion since the mid-1970s. The civilian movement was repressed, and in 2003 the government mounted a full-scale offensive with tens of thousands more troops (Reid 2006; Drexler 2008; Aspinall 2009; Miller 2009; Barter 2014). In West Papua, known as Irian Jaya under the New Order, a civilian independence movement, in addition to the longstanding poorly armed guerrillas of the Free Papua Movement (Organisasi Papua Merdeka), emerged with demonstrations, popular congresses, ceremonial raisings of the independence's Morning Star flag, and extensive human rights violations by the Indonesian military.[15] These abuses included the murder of independence leaders, shootings, and mass arrests (Rutherford & Mote 2001).

Unlike this separatist-related violence, which many had anticipated with regime change, intercommunal bloodshed in the outer islands shocked the country and its observers. Local scrambles over the control of decentralization's resources sparked massive ethnic violence in Ambon (Moluccas), North Moluccas, Poso (Central Sulawesi), Sambas (West Kalimantan), and Sampit (Central Kalimantan) (Bertrand 2004; Wilson 2011; McRae 2013; Duncan 2013). Religious polarization also inflamed tensions in places

---

[15] Presently, the Indonesian half of the island New Guinea comprises two provinces, Papua and West Papua. Because the people of these provinces overwhelmingly refer themselves as West Papuans and their territory as West Papua, I use their terminology.

(Sidel 2006), although less so for the bouts of violence on Kalimantan (Davidson 2008). While geographically concentrated, these communal clashes claimed the lives of more than 6,000 Indonesians and displaced in excess of another million (inclusive of separatist-related violence) (Varshney, Tadjoeddin, & Panggabean 2008; Hedman 2008). Clashes tended to break out in provinces where local economies were heavily dependent on the state sector and in electorally uncompetitive districts (van Klinken 2007; Toha 2017).

## 2.2 Political Economy

Indonesians drove their country's political liberalization; in the realm of economic reforms, they were not in the lead. That the International Monetary Fund (IMF) hijacked the process explains to a degree the resistance that arose against the recovery program. It also stoked hostility to economic liberalization.

More so than any country affected by the 1997/8 Asian Financial Crisis, Indonesia experienced not one but two crises. Soeharto's regime was destabilized by an economic meltdown.[16] In 1998, the economy contracted by more than 13 percent; the rupiah, Indonesia's currency, at one point lost 90 percent of its value; business bankruptcies soared; capital flight, estimated in the billions of dollars, ensued; and millions of Indonesians who had been lifted from poverty were thrust back into despair. On import-dependent Java, as the construction sector and urban economies ground to a halt, millions returned to villages desperate to find work in the informal sector or on tiny rice farms (Breman 2001; Lont & White 2003). This gloom contrasted with some outer-island areas where exporters of commodities such as cocoa, fresh fruit, and spices experienced a windfall since the slide in the rupiah made their products more attractive internationally. The economic rupture was extraordinary. In a region that suffered economic collapse, only Indonesia recorded negative rates of foreign direct investment for a number of years following the onset of the crisis (Aswicahyono, Hill, & Narjoko 2010).

In exchange for billions in bailout loans, Indonesia's cash-strapped government was forced to agree to strict IMF conditionality measures. The IMF, a US-controlled organization, used the crisis as a pretext to pry open what was only a partially protected economy. Notwithstanding the strong rates of growth Soeharto's economic governance system had produced, the IMF now sought to eliminate monopolies and other cronyistic practices that it believed blocked the further integration of the domestic economy with world trade.

---

[16] For a succinct summary of the causes of the Asian Financial Crisis, see Hill (2000, 272–4).

The fate of Bulog, Indonesia's State Logistic Board, graphically illustrates what happened to some of the monopolies that had nurtured vast rent-seeking schemes and patronage networks. The IMF forced the government to revoke Bulog's rice import monopoly. The move proved disastrous, however: without a regulatory framework in place, record amounts of foreign rice soon flooded the Indonesian market, and domestic rice prices failed to fall as market theory had predicted (Sawit & Lokollo 2007). The lack of institutional safeguards also facilitated the disappearance of billions of US dollars from the Bank of Indonesia, the central bank; money that was intended to recapitalize the country's flagging banking sector. (Nonperforming loans were a problem even before the crisis). The IMF-inspired Indonesian Bank Restructuring Authority – which closed and took over troubled banks, rescheduled debt payments, and sold distressed assets – had little power to stem the outflow of funds.[17] It was true there was some support for the IMF's program among the technocrats of various ministries, and some of Soeharto's cronies and his children lost valuable rents. Yet, without a thorough change in key government personnel, predatory interests continued to prosper. Beneficiaries included ethnic Chinese owners of massive conglomerates and native Indonesian politico-businessmen alike. Certainly, few among Indonesia's party establishment wanted to see the IMF reform program succeed (Robison & Hadiz 2004).

Undaunted, the IMF pushed ahead. One prong of its program was the privatization of state assets. In 1999, the government reached only two-thirds of its negotiated privatization target of US$1.5 billion, because elements in the bureaucracy, parliament, and the business class obstructed the process (Rosser 2002, 186–7). Most privatizations that were carried out were only partial, with minority shares floated on Jakarta's stock exchange. These included state companies in the construction, banking, and telecommunication sectors, and the national airline, Garuda.

Over time, the international financial institutions also sought to safeguard or institutionalize changes, known as the "second generation" of reforms (World Bank 2005). Market liberalization could be easily achieved by the stroke of an executive's pen, but it could also be revoked just as easily by a countervailing executive order of a succeeding president. Without institutional lock-in, a main takeaway from the influential New Institutional Economics literature, the certainty investors crave is lacking (North 1990). Uncertainty deters investors

---

[17] The agency had some success in consolidating the banking sector, slashing nearly in half the number of commercial banks and their collective balance of outstanding loans (Sato 2005, 93).

from investing in long-term productive assets, crippling sustainable growth. New Institutional Economics posits that increased investor confidence stems from domestic formal institutions that promote efficiency, enhance the credibility of economic policies, tie the grabbing hands of government, and protect private property rights. As importantly, institutional safeguards need to protect markets from predatory elites who exploit market power through collusion with government officials and from overwhelming societal demand – for example, the misallocation of resources to satisfy a pivotal political constituency. In all, the institutionalization of regulatory safeguards, combined with market liberalization, is often associated with the concept of good economic governance.[18] Economists, however, disagree over the appropriate mix of free markets and regulatory institutions. The exact ingredients of good economic governance remain contentious – just like that of democracy.

A professional judiciary that can impartially adjudicate disputes over contracts and property rights is an oft cited example of an endogenous, growth-enhancing, formal institution (Posner 1998). With Indonesia's Supreme Court in a state of disrepair, the IMF, along with donor counterparts, prompted the formation of a Commercial Court in 1998. A clean and responsible specialized court, it was hoped, could aid foreign creditors in recovering assets sunk in domestic firms that were now declared bankrupt. The nakedness of the IMF's intent – to recover investors' funds rather than genuinely try to bolster the institutional foundation for a good governance program – perhaps doomed this effort from the outset. Initial Commercial Court cases, epitomized by the dubious insolvency ruling of a local subsidiary of a Canadian insurance company, were marred by corruption accusations (Bedner 2008). Another example of institutional lock-in was the passage by parliament, in 1999, of an antimonopoly (or competition) law. Although the law was mandated by the government's agreements with the IMF, there was support for it among parliamentarians. They saw it as a means to prevent the domination of the country's economy by massive conglomerates, as had dominated the economy during the New Order. How committed parliament was to the pro-market policies the law was intended to promote, however, was not clear at the time. The 1999 act also mandated the establishment of a specialized regulatory agency – the Business Competition Supervisory Commission. Like much legislation in Indonesia, the statute was riven with conflicting and vaguely worded provisions, which impeded the commission's ability to effectively adjudicate cases. Lastly, in

---

[18] This is also known as the post-Washington Consensus. While liberalization and regulation historically and ideologically make odd bedfellows, they have become complementary pieces in reform prescriptions to rid developing countries of corruption and patrimonialism (Jayasuriya 2005).

2003 parliament promulgated a statute on fiscal responsibility, mandating that the Finance Ministry – that is, technocrats and not politicians – keep a tight watch on fiscal deficits. Deficits by law are now disallowed from surpassing 2 percent of gross domestic product, thereby strengthening the credibility of anti-inflationary policies (Aswicahyono, Bird, & Hill 2009).

Beyond these innovations, the IMF and the World Bank promoted a broad campaign of statutory liberalization paired with regulation in vital economic sectors. Legislation focused on telecommunications (1999), oil and natural gas (2001), electricity (2002), water (2004), forests (2004), and roads (2004). Taken together, these statutes were intended to signal policy continuity and credible commitment to market-based competition. This was deemed crucial by the multilateral organizations because of both the weakness of the rule of law in Indonesia and the vicissitudes of democratic elections, where a change in government could induce substantial changes in policy (Davidson 2015a).

Things did not go according the plans of the multilateral organizations, however. Harsh conditionality measures helped to stoke antagonistic economic nationalism. Its ascent influenced a series of policy changes and court rulings against foreign interests. In late 2003, for instance, Megawati's government terminated its conditionality program with the IMF ahead of schedule. In the following year, the Constitutional Court struck down the law that liberalized the electricity sector, a blow to foreign investors who were prevalent in this field.[19]

The Asian Financial Crisis did, however, present an opportunity to loosen the (mostly ethnic Chinese) conglomerates' grip on the economy that many Indonesians resented. At the same time, the crisis stoked fears that foreign capitalists would swallow up corporate assets at fire-sale prices. Notably, the Salim group, once Southeast Asia's largest conglomerate, lost control over its most prized asset (The Bank of Central Asia). The family, however, retained ownership over its lucrative foods division (Borsuk & Chng 2014). Foreign investment did become considerable in the banking sector; both the Malaysian and Singapore governments invested heavily in some of Indonesia's larger banks (Carney & Hamilton-Hart 2015). But the domestic conglomerates remained powerful – with the New Order gone they now possessed more direct access to party elites and government officials, which resulted in more

---

[19] Civil society groups charged that these liberalizing laws were mostly about privatization and violated the peoples' economy clause of the 1945 Constitution [33(3)] that mandates state control over vital resources. These organizations brought a number of cases in front of the Constitutional Court to get a ruling on their constitutionality (Butt & Lindsey 2008).

autonomy (Chua 2008; Fukuoka 2012). Foreign domination of Indonesia's economy did not come to pass.

Lastly, words are required on how the uncertainty of the transition and a weakened central government affected outer-island economies. Decentralization facilitated implementation of some innovative policies, but these were largely limited to a handful of specific urban locales (von Luebke 2009). More generally, decentralization spurred a frenzied dash of gold rush-like proportions. Illegal logging and mining boomed. Legal extractions also grew apace as empowered district heads (*bupati*) distributed thousands of small-scale licenses. On the ground, amid rapacious digging and cutting, there was little clarity about who owned what; already weak under the New Order, property rights further deteriorated. Overlapping claims of multiple actors mounted year by year. There were large companies with licenses from New Order days, illegal operators backed by powerful local elites, indigenous communities, other locals although not "indigenous" to the area, wealthier migrants looking to exploit rising commodity prices, and new concession holders unconstrained by the strictures of their licenses. It seemed to matter little whether the exploitation took place in resource-rich or resource-poor areas; actors clashed and cooperated with little regard for the law or the environment (Li 2001; Casson & Obidzinski 2002; McCarthy 2002, 2004; Gellert 2010; Erb 2016; Peluso 2018). Meanwhile, with minimal institutional capacity to raise revenue autonomously, some local governments resorted to levying road taxes on transportation ferrying legal and illegally obtained goods (LPEM-FEUI & Asian Foundation 2009). In sum, while political scientists have praised decentralization for the political centripetalism it has fostered across the archipelago (Aspinall 2010; Horowitz 2013; Mietzner 2014a), economists have regarded it as growth-retarding (McLeod 2005; Aswichahyono, Bird, & Hill 2009).[20]

## 2.3 Identity-Based Mobilizations

The transition period also sparked significant "innovations" in the way identity-based groups coalesced and mobilized. Three of the more consequential of them were groups acutely marginalized by decades of authoritarian rule. Let us examine them one by one.

### 2.3.1 Conservative Islam

While Soeharto's army had annihilated the left in the 1960s, it equally did not tolerate mobilizations on the right – that is, by puritanical Islam (Feillard &

---

[20] Pepinsky and Wihardja (2011) found decentralization's impact on national growth to have been net neutral.

Madinier 2010; Laffan 2011; Formichi 2012). Yet, over time, events external and internal to the country made the "Islam question" harder to ignore. One external development was the global growth of a strictly orthodox Sunni movement within Islam; in particular, the pumping of Saudi petro-dollars throughout the Muslim world starting in the 1970s facilitated the spread of Wahhabism, a doctrine and movement that venerates the time of the Prophet Mohammad in the seventh century. Soon thereafter, the 1979 Iranian Revolution elevated the status of Islam, and particularly Shi'ism, as a geopolitical force. By the 1980s within Indonesia, economic growth created a Muslim middle class that began to demand more Islamic-oriented policies and public and private institutions. And as Soeharto's inner circle aged, he exploited this rise in Islamic public religiosity to corral a new support base (Liddle 1996; Effendy 2003). His 1991 *haj* pilgrimage to Mecca reflected this tilt.

On the whole, radical Islamic groups were contained – some were coopted – rather than eliminated as happened to the Indonesian Communist Party. For example, inspired by the Egyptian Muslim Brotherhood, a movement of Islamic study groups (*Tarbiyah*) proliferated on university campuses. But because of repressive campus environments, they kept a low profile. Discussions focused on personal piety and purification of the faith, on the writings of (foreign) modernist reformers, and on the irreconcilability between the state ideology of *Pancasila* (Five Precepts) and authentic Islam.[21] In the late New Order, these groups took advantage of the new space afforded by Soeharto's tilt to Islam to protest against the injustices Muslims suffered in Bosnia and Palestine (but less so in Aceh). After Soeharto fell, and railing against all things American, Zionist, and liberal within Indonesia, Wahhabi and related Salafi groups, including the Indonesian Liberation Party (Hizbut Tahrir Indonesia, HTI), further blossomed on account of the freedoms that a democratic and decentralized Indonesia presented (Hefner 2000; van Bruinessen 2002).[22] Alongside their promotion of puritanical reformism, these groups also displayed strong transnational orientations (unlike Nahdlatul Ulama and Muhammadiyah) (van Bruinessen 2013a).

Some Islamists sought electoral success as a means to Islamize Indonesian politics and society after Soeharto's fall. Control of government, for example, would aid in enforcing the Jakarta Charter, which would oblige all Muslims to live according to the precepts of Islamic law (*shari`a*). New Islamist parties

---

[21] The five precepts are: 1) belief in one God; 2) universal humanity; 3) national unity; 4) consultative democracy; and 5) social justice.

[22] It should be stressed that these groups did not participate actively in Soeharto's overthrow.

fared poorly, however, in the 1999 elections. The Justice Party and the Moon and Star Party, two of the most prominent, each received less than 2 percent of the vote. This disappointment convinced some Islamists that the path to revolutionary change lay in extralegal means.

This path meant, among other things, more mass demonstrations. Attacking liberal democracy and liberal influences within mainstream Indonesian Islam, protesters demanded the enactment of the aforementioned Jakarta Charter and vilified Megawati's presidency. Protests prompted violence. New youth militias, such as the Islamic Defenders Front (Front Pembela Islam, FPI), raided bars and cafés in Jakarta and other cities as symbols of vice and Western, liberal lifestyles. Another youth militia, Laskar Jihad (Holy Warriors), sent members to fight alongside fellow Muslims in Ambon and in Poso in their battle against local Christians (Hassan 2006). Unemployment, underemployment, and disillusionment among the urban youth, along with participation in gangster-like activities, aided militia recruitment (Wilson 2015).

The militias did not act alone. They drew support from financially endowed and established ultra-conservative organizations such as the Indonesian Islamic Predication Council and its spin-off organization, the Indonesian Committee for Solidarity with the Muslim World. There were also more controversial connections to elements of the state. Jakarta's police, for example, used the raids on cafés by Islamic militia as a way to increase the amount of protection money the businesses were paying them. Cliques in the security forces facilitated the transport of Laskar Jihad fighters to eastern Indonesia to destabilize Gus Dur's administration (S. Jones 2013).

Yet, when other radical groups such as Jemaah Islamiyah, which seeks to establish a (supranational) Islamic caliphate in Indonesia, began a bombing campaign after the 9/11 attacks in the United States, the thesis of Indonesian state complicity became harder to sustain. Jemaah Islamiyah targeted churches in more than ten Indonesian cities on Christmas Eve in 2000; nightclubs in Bali in 2002 in which more than 200 people, mainly Australians and Indonesians, died; the Marriot Hotel in Jakarta in 2003; and the Australian Embassy in 2004, to name just four incidents. Subsequently, Jemaah Islamiyah broadened its network to conflict zones in southern Thailand and the southern Philippines. Within Indonesia, its operations eventually dwindled in scale and in number due to both internal organizational debates over killing civilian Indonesian Muslims and due to enhanced Indonesian security (S. Jones 2013).[23] But Jemaah Islamiyah's emergence and the violence it perpetrated stoked alarmist

---

[23] Australia in particular significantly aided Indonesia's counterterrorist police units. On why some jihadists quit, see Hwang (2018).

fear among Western intelligence agencies about the possible links to and the expansion of al-Qaeda into Southeast Asia (Hamilton-Hart 2006; Sidel 2006).

During the early transition period, a minority of Indonesia's Muslims supported puritanical reformism; the majority would have rejected turning Indonesia into an Islamic state. That said, in fueling over time a widespread "conservative turn" within Indonesian Muslim society, these movements have inescapably influenced the country (van Bruinessen 2013a).

### 2.3.2 Chinese Indonesians

One domestic source of the resurgence of conservative Islam was its interaction with and reaction to other identity groups. Few have been as prominent as the Indonesians of Chinese descent, although they comprise only 2–3 percent of the country's population. Tension between the two collective identity groups, Muslims and Chinese, is not new. An early and significant Islamic nationalist organization, Sarekat Dagang Islam (Islamic Traders Union), was formed in Central Java in the early twentieth century by Islamic batik merchants to bolster collective efforts against ethnic Chinese competitors (Shiraishi 1990). Discriminatory government policies – notably a 1959 law that prohibited Chinese merchants from trading in villages – and anti-Chinese violence are also decades old, at least (Mackie 1976).[24]

The New Order regime borrowed colonial techniques to address the so-called Chinese question. Illustratively, it encouraged capital accumulation among a select few to extract resources from them, while politically repressing the community as a whole (Anderson 1983). The New Order also used its anticommunist platform as a pretext for widespread discrimination, given communist China's looming regional presence. The regime's policy of forced assimilation featured the banning (formal and informal) of Chinese schools, Confucianism as a religion, and the public display of Chinese writing. Even the official designation of "Chinese" in Indonesian ("*Cina*") was derogatory (Coppel 1983).[25]

As the movement behind political Islam gained momentum in the late New Order, violence committed against Chinese property, also associated with Christian ownership, rose in towns across Java (Sidel 2006). But these incidents did not portend the scale of the violence perpetrated against ethnic Chinese in May 1998. Although conflict also broke out in the cities of Medan (North Sumatra) and Solo (Central Java), the worst of it erupted in Jakarta,

---

[24] Ethnic Chinese, however, were not the primary targets of the 1965–66 anticommunist massacres contrary to prevailing understandings outside Indonesia (Cribb & Coppel 2009).

[25] This term can be rendered as "chink" in English.

where scores of rapes of ethnic Chinese women were reported. Deaths topped 1,000, although the majority comprised young looters trapped in Chinese-owned stores and buildings that were set alight. Thousands of better-off ethnic Chinese fled to neighboring Singapore, at least (for some) temporarily. But for these communities, as in so many other aspects of Indonesian life, the events of May 1998 proved to be a momentous turning point.

With the passing of this horrific episode, and with political Islam's attention turned toward state capture, large-scale attacks against the Chinese dissipated (Sidel 2006).[26] Remarkably, by the time the 1999 election campaigns kicked off, the holding of lion and dragon dances had become a staple at rallies of secular parties trying to attract Chinese voters (Budianta 2007). Some minor Chinese parties were formed, and although they did not achieve much electoral success, they indicated the growing political confidence of some Indonesian Chinese (Suryadinata 2001).

Soon thereafter, the informal shift in the treatment of Indonesian Chinese was made official. Gus Dur's administration (October 1999–July 2001) lifted the New Order ban on public displays of Chinese writing and recognized Confucianism as the state's sixth official religion. Taking advantage of greater press and civil society freedoms, Chinese language publications and voluntary organizations also mushroomed (Hoon 2008). The flourishing of Chinese communities also has been aided by external influences, notably the rise of China. Relations between Indonesia and China have been troubled since Soeharto destroyed the Indonesian Communist Party and pursued a strict program of discrimination against Indonesian Chinese. But as China's economic star rose, urban Chinese and non-Chinese students in post-Soeharto Indonesia have since flocked to Chinese-language tuition centers, amplifying the upswing in China's cultural "soft" power. Yet, in hindsight, the period's excitement – like that about democracy more generally – fed unrealistic expectations of the country having once and for all lain to rest its Chinese question.

### 2.3.3 Revival of Tradition in the Outer Islands[27]

The post-Soeharto renaissance of conservative Islam and Chinese Indonesians did not take observers by surprise. The rise and demands of a third identity collective – outer-island, marginalized ethnic groups seeking empowerment through a revival of tradition – did. Unlike the other two identity movements,

---

[26] Disappointingly, but not surprisingly, the state failed to prosecute perpetrators of the May 1998 violence (Purdey 2006).

[27] This section draws from Henley and Davidson (2008) unless stated otherwise.

this traditionalist mobilization has placed ties to or conflict over land at the center of its struggle. Indigenous leadership and activism were often created in the crucible of opposition to land expropriation by state and private pulp, paper, and timber companies in Sumatra, large oil-palm plantations in Kalimantan, or mining interests in West Papua. The New Order had ignored the nonstate, collective rights these groups claimed over ancestral land and resources. As a result, these groups began to promote tradition – *adat* – as a complex of rights and obligations tying history, land, and law together in a way that appears specific to Indonesia, at least in a Southeast Asian context. The essence of this linkage is that laws and rights are historical inheritances rather than an artifact of government, that the most important domain of law is the control of land, and that the historical control of land is in turn the most important source of land rights. The New Order regime disagreed. It cited state law, which emphasizes state control of land, as specified by the still existing 1960 Basic Agrarian Law. New Order elites thus saw the sparsely populated lands as empty but valuable spaces to be logged or dug up for the precious minerals they contained, or alternatively as dumping grounds for migrants from land-crowded Java.

The *adat* revival has been concentrated either in areas where the progress of Islam was blocked by Christianity or Hinduism, or where Islamic conversion took place but pre-Islamic elements remained unusually important in social life (as in West Sumatra among the Minangkabau ethnic group). But this identity mobilization has shared key features with conservative Islam and Chinese Indonesians; below, I enumerate three of them. The first is how the *adat* movement has grappled with the historical legacies of colonial policy. As in their containment of Islam or in their construction of the Chinese as distinct economic subjects, the Dutch saw these ethno-linguistic groups as discrete, genuine collectivities. Moreover, they were conceived as receptacles of authentically Indonesian (that is, pre-Islamic) cultural groups who governed themselves by laws and tradition distinctly different from the so-called West. To some Dutch administrators, their systems of traditional law (*hukum adat*) should be respected, if not for ideological reasons then at least as a means to protect these vulnerable groups from the ravages of land-hungry Dutch capitalists. This thinking – and the concomitant split among colonial officials – contributed to the development of the well-known concept of legal pluralism pursued by the Netherlands Indies government.

The second similarity between the *adat* movement and both the Indonesian Chinese and conservative Islamic mobilizations has been the pivotal role played by transnational influences. The *adat* movement was inspired by and has enjoyed the support of international organizations and networks committed to the rights of indigenous peoples, the preservation of cultural diversity, and the idea that community and tradition can help protect the natural environment. In the last decades of the twentieth century, a growing postmodern disillusionment with universalistic models of human progress, including grand political projects such as nationalism and socialism, led to a new sympathy in the rich countries for the predicament of underprivileged groups defined essentially by ethnicity and indigeneity rather than poverty, class, or nationality. At the same time, environmentalist movements were emerging as guardians of a new type of political idealism to replace the old egalitarian idealism of the left. Today, access to an indigenous identity in practice can be determined by familiarity with the international discourse and politics of indigenous rights as much as by ancestry, culture, or marginality (Li 2000). In Indonesia, the indigenous peoples' federation called the Archipelagic Alliance of Adat Communities (Aliansi Masyarakat Adat Nusantara) has been the frequent recipient of foreign donor funding and has been an effective user of international media. The federation has also been involved in such international indigenous rights advocacy organizations as the International Working Group on Indigenous Affairs (Copenhagen) and the Asia Indigenous Peoples Pact, a Thailand-based confederation established in 1992.[28]

The third striking similarity is that the early *adat* mobilizations were a direct critique of New Order rule and its style of governance. Movement leaders have sought to exploit the opportunities democratization and decentralization have provided to foster the protection, empowerment, and mobilization of under-privileged groups. In some places, this has meant the acceptance of migrants, both new and longstanding, into local society (Bräuchler 2017). Unfortunately, the *adat* movement has also spawned anti-migrant attacks. Much of the violence in West Kalimantan and Central Kalimantan, for example, involved indigenous Dayaks asserting what they regard as traditional rights of territorial control against the interests of the state and its cronies. Attacks were perpetrated, however, against poor migrants from Madura Island, located off the coast of East Java (Davidson 2008). *Adat* served here and elsewhere as a rationale for ethnic exclusion and a justification for ethnic violence.[29] Thankfully, as Indonesia's innovative transition gave way to stagnation – the

---

[28] A key development occurred when, in 1989, the International Labor Organization passed its Convention 169, the first international instrument to reject the assimilationist approach to indigenous populations.

[29] It has also been seen as an important, if problematic, mechanism for reconciliation (Davidson 2007; Bräuchler 2009).

subject of the next section – much of this bloodshed receded. Erstwhile aggressors, capitalizing on their gains made in the sociocultural realm, began turning their attention toward the capture of political and economic resources controlled by the state or otherwise.

## 3 Stagnation

Perhaps it was inevitable that the euphoria of the early reform period would breed fatigue and frustration. After all, Soeharto was not overthrown by a movement of revolutionary change. Few expected, though, that reforms would stagnate so briskly under Indonesia's first directly elected president, Susilo Bambang Yudhoyono, a former general but self-professed reformer. The large political parties colluded among themselves to write the rules of the game in their favor and to guard their access to lucrative state-controlled rents. Yudhoyono remained beholden to their rapacity, even when he was reelected in 2009. But he did govern during a period of relative prosperity. Not only was the economy on a slow, steady mend from the 1997/8 crisis, but his time in office also coincided with a dramatic commodity boom fueled by thriving demand from China and India. Indonesia's protectionist politico-business elites thus were afforded the means by which to dodge IMF policy prescriptions – amassing staggering riches while exploiting (if not instigating) a wave of economic nationalism to mask their avarice.

While inequality widened, a more financially stout state was able to blunt its impact by implementing social safety-net programs, which poor Indonesians-cum-voters appreciated. Neither job creation nor investment in infrastructure, however, kept pace. A pernicious form of decentralized corruption also took hold. Elected regional heads, some of whom controlled vast resources, challenged the authority of arrogant and pious central government officials. At least local electioneering and sharing of spoils helped to mollify combatants, and the death toll along the country's periphery declined considerably. Moving in the opposite direction, however, was the surge of political Islam, expanding its influence deeper into the domains of formal politics and economic policymaking.

### 3.1 Politics

By acceding to direct presidential elections, as covered in Section 2, the established party elite interjected a degree of uncertainty into Indonesia's political landscape. This indeterminacy bore fruit when in 2004 Susilo Bambang Yudhoyono, leading the new Democrat Party (Partai Demokrat) convincingly defeated Megawati in a second-round runoff for the presidency.

The established party elite had mistakenly thought their supporters would follow instructions on whom to vote for. Yudhoyono was not a true outsider, however. He had been a New Order general and a minister in Gus Dur's and Megawati's cabinets. But few envisaged that a new party could capture the presidency so swiftly. Lacking a strong political party machine, Yudhoyono rode to victory on his security background, his reformist image, his perceived internationalism, and his telegenic looks (Honna 2012). His vice-presidential pick of Jusuf Kalla, a devout Muslim who hails from Sulawesi and a longtime Golkar stalwart, ensured that eastern Indonesia's then most popular party (Golkar) would support his presidency. It also signaled, at least superficially, that outer-island interests would be represented at the highest heights of the Indonesian government.

Held prior to the historic presidential election, the 2004 legislative election had already shown that the Indonesian electorate was getting fed up with politics-as-usual and was seeking alternatives elsewhere, which included refraining from voting altogether.[30] Vote totals for each of the big five parties experienced a decline from their 1999 outcomes, with their accumulative total dipping by more than 20 percent. Their dismal showing raised at least three questions: 1) To which parties were voters switching their allegiances?; 2) Why was this happening?; and 3) How did established parties respond to this shift?

Above we noted that the Democrat Party was one beneficiary of changing voter preferences. Building on Yudhoyono's 2004 presidential victory, it improved on its showing in the 2004 legislative elections to garner almost 21 percent of the votes in the 2009 contest to become the largest party in parliament. As a presidential, catch-all party, the Democrat Party lured voters away from the secular-nationalist parties of Golkar and PDI-P, but the party's grassroots efforts to heed Islamic concerns resonated among Islamic voters too (Hassan 2013).

A new conservative party, the Islamist Prosperous Justice Party (Partai Keadilan Sejahtera, PKS), was also a beneficiary. As noted in Section 2.3.1, the predecessor of PKS, the Justice Party, fared poorly in the 1999 election; so, the 7.3 percent garnered by PKS in 2004 was both impressive and unexpected. Its success could be traced to the nascent rise of hardline Islam and the party's anticorruption stance. For its backing of Yudhoyono in the 2004 presidential election, the president awarded PKS three cabinet positions, including the lucrative Agriculture portfolio. (It was given four upon Yudhoyono's 2009 reelection).

---

[30] From a high of 99 percent in 1999, voter turnout in the legislative elections progressively declined to 75 percent by 2014. This latter figure undercounts the true number because it does not take into account the number of purposely spoiled ballots.

As PKS rose to electoral prominence, it too became a popular topic of research. Scholars explored the party's meritocratic cadre and recruitment system and its social welfare work among constituents. Yet the party's rise in relation to the "inclusion-moderation" thesis piqued the most academic interest. The thesis maintains that through the bargaining and negotiation inherent to electoral democracy, hardliners learn cooperative behavior and thus moderate their attitudes, behavior, and ideologies. For some, this thesis seemingly was at work because PKS went on to enter into electoral coalitions with secular parties at the local levels. Moreover, the party no longer insists on applying the Jakarta Charter – obliging Muslims to follow *shari`a* or Islamic law – to Indonesia's constitution. Yet debate over the Jakarta Charter also caused a rift within the party: A conservative faction has insisted that its implementation anchor the party's platform. The rift hurt the party electorally, as its 2009 vote total scarcely budged upward (Bubalo & Fealy 2005; Machmudi 2008; Hwang 2010; Hamayotsu 2011; Tomsa 2012; Tanuwidjaja 2012; Hicks 2012; Buehler 2013; Menchik 2016; Park n.d.).

The second question addresses why this shift toward newer parties was happening. Certainly, growing social forces, notably the rise of conservative Islam, were making inroads at the ballot box. But other factors were at work too. The one-time dominant view in Indonesia had held that affiliation with a particular socio-religious identity or stream (*aliran*) determined one's political preference (Geertz 1960). But based on survey data of voter behavior between the 1999 and 2004 elections, one important study concluded that the interactive influences of urbanization, party leader personalities, and mass media were eroding the effectiveness of *aliran* attachments (Liddle & Mujani 2007). Such findings, however, may not bode well for the long-term prospects of Indonesia's party system. If the healthy social rootedness of parties ebbs, this might destabilize the system, weakening and fragmenting until it resembles those found in the Philippines and Thailand (Tan 2015[31]). This destabilization – what political scientists call dealignment – had already begun, especially in eastern Indonesia. There small parties, driven by efforts to capture state resources for patronage purposes, were coalescing and thus eroding Golkar's longtime dominant position. This was occurring in particular in districts with state-dependent economies (Allen 2014; Tomsa 2014).

---

[31] Weakly institutionalized parties in these two countries suffer from rampant party-switching by opportunistic politicians. That the dominant religion there is more institutionally centralized – Catholicism in the Philippines, Buddhism in Thailand – as compared to the decentralized structure of Islam might account for a degree of this divergence among their party systems (Ufen 2008).

The worry of the big parties over dealignment leads to the third question: what was their response to their declining electoral fortunes? Most prominently, they have ensured that they and not an independent electoral commission control the rulemaking process for the country's party and electoral systems (Reilly 2006; Choi 2012).[32] In short, the established parties write rules in their favor that hamper pesky upstarts. To illustrate, the requirements to be recognized as a "national party" in order to compete in national elections have been progressively raised. As a result, the number of parties that were allowed to run in 2004 was cut in half from the forty-eight that participated in the 1999 ballot. Parliament also raised the electoral threshold from 2 percent to 2.5 percent for the 2004 ballot, making it more difficult for new parties to win seats in the national parliament.

Large parties maintain that such constraints enhance parliamentary governance. A profusion of parties, they say, makes the legislative process unwieldy and cumbersome. This reasoning, however, glosses over naked party interests in excluding new, smaller parties from accessing state-controlled rents. Instead, corruption, the parties' antiquated use of information, and their emphasis on decision-making based on consensus rather than voting have contributed to parliament's sluggish legislative output (Ziegenhain 2008; Sherlock 2010).

Although normally competing with one another, the main parties have proven capable of acting in concert when their collective interests have been threatened. The requirements to be deemed a national party and the rising electoral threshold were two instances. A third institutional tweak has been the rules governing presidential election candidature. For the 2004 inaugural contest, only parties with at least 5 percent of the votes or with 3 percent of parliament's seats were eligible to nominate candidates. Smaller parties thus were forced to join forces with larger parties. For the 2009 election, in which Yudhoyono again defeated Megawati but this time by a wide enough first-round margin to avoid a runoff,[33] the rules for nomination were stiffened to require a party or coalition to have a minimum of one-quarter of the popular vote or one-fifth of seats in parliament. Put simply, the major parties have ensured that they remain king- or queen-makers in the quest for Indonesia's most coveted political prize: the presidency.

---

[32] The mandate and duties of the independent electoral commission are restricted to the implementation of such rules.

[33] Yudhyono's reelection was helped considerably by his administration's timely distribution of direct cash subsidies to millions of eligible voters that was promoted as an antipoverty measure.

The overwhelming consensus is that Yudhoyono's two presidencies (2004–9, 2009–14) were disappointing (Liddle 2013; Aspinall, Mietzner & Tomsa 2015). Save for the peace agreement reached in Aceh – which happened after the massive tsunami of December 2014 that slammed into the province's west and north coasts and killed more than 200,000 people – Yudhoyono achieved few breakthroughs.[34] Political reforms stagnated. Corruption among political parties continued, if not worsened, under his watch. Graft among the established parties has been longstanding. Then scandals broke out among two new parties with hitherto clean reputations – Yudhoyono's own Democrat Party in 2012 and PKS in 2013 (recall the latter's multiple cabinet positions). These scandals only served to reinforce the conventional wisdom that the country's parties are more interested in patronage than policy and more steeped in the ways of corruption than swayed by ideology (Fionna 2014). Encouragingly, voters at least made Yudhoyono's party pay for its indiscretions. Its vote tally in 2014 was slashed by about half from its 2009 total of 21 percent. From being the largest party in parliament, it fell to the fourth largest. Nor was the Democrat Party able to field a candidate in the vice- or presidential slots for the 2014 presidential election.

Others interpreted the corruption scandals differently. Mietzner (2013) has sought to show in comparative context how parties in young, patronage democracies face similar problems, such as weak party identification, and that Indonesia's parties are more institutionalized than conventional wisdom allows. Mietzner blames the state's refusal to subsidize parties for their desperate scramble over lucrative cabinet positions (see also Fionna 2013).

Party corruption – or whatever one prefers to call it – also affected Yudhoyono's ambivalent attitude toward the country's new Corruption Eradication Commission. As part of the transition's repertoire of institutional innovation, the commission was formed to combat Indonesia's notorious corruption problem. It was accorded wide-ranging coordinating, supervising, investigating, and monitoring duties along with some prosecutorial powers. Operational since 2003, the anticorruption body hit its stride in 2008 with prosecutions of a number of high-ranking officials. Instead of backing the agency, the president's support wavered at critical times. This was most evident when the commission began investigating members of the security apparatus and the political party establishment (Butt 2015; Schütte 2017). Because the agency's achievements spawned anti-reformist counterattacks, civil society

---

[34] Even here as much credit for the peace accord was given to his vice president, Jusuf Kalla.

had to rush to the commission's defense in the court of public opinion (Mietzner 2012).

Military reforms also stalled under Yudhoyono. As a former general, he held enough sway to keep officers from overstepping bounds into civilian affairs. Yet he did not utilize this sway to push for further regularization of the military's finances; nor did he dismantle the military's business networks. Thus, the goal that the military be fully financed by the state by 2009, as mandated by the 2004 law on the matter, went unmet (Human Rights Watch 2010). Attempts to hold both high- and low-ranking officers accountable in civilian courts fared even worse. So did reforms elsewhere, such as efforts at agrarian renewal (Rachman 2017) and improvements among law-and-order institutions (Isra 2014). These turned out to be empty campaign promises.

There were several reasons behind the Yudhoyono-led stagnation. The president suffered from outsized expectations. After all, he won the country's inaugural direct presidential election and followed this historic victory with an even more convincing reelection. While he ran on an anticorruption and reformist platform, too much was expected of him to solve the many ills of Indonesian political society. The office of the presidency had been weakened by design, and this task was too onerous for an individual. Some cited Yudhoyono's cautious personality and fear of making difficult decisions (Fealy 2015), but structural factors also played their part. With only 10 percent of the seats in parliament in 2004 and roughly one-quarter in 2009, the Democrat Party needed a broad, perhaps unruly, coalition to govern. Thus, the collusive feature of party politics continued largely unabated (with the exception that the PDI-P did not join the ruling coalition, largely because Megawati remained angered that Yudhoyono had broken his promise not to run against her). In an interview, Yudhoyono mentioned the necessity of juggling multiple, competing interests, which complicated governance (Aspinall, Mietzner & Tomsa 2015). He prioritized stability. Stated differently, he privileged the status quo and not democratic reforms. Whatever Yudhoyono's faults were in the political realm, they were as conspicuous, if not more so, in managing the country's economy.

## 3.2 Political Economy

Stagnation might be an unduly harsh way to describe Indonesia's economic performance under Yudhoyono. Economic growth rates averaged about 5.5 percent per annum, far outpacing growth in the economies of the USA

(1.8 percent), Japan (0.8 percent), and the countries of the Euro currency area (1.0 percent) over the same period.[35] Indonesia's poverty rate also fell steadily from 16 percent in 2007 to 11 percent in 2014.[36]

Then again, China's economy annually expanded some 10 percent, and Vietnam's 6.5 percent over the same period. While perhaps outliers, both of these countries lifted tens of millions of people out of poverty. Economists are also rather skeptical of Indonesia's official poverty figures. Using different methodologies from those of the Indonesian government, the Asian Development Bank estimates that the number of poor is nearly twice the official tally. This would mean that, as of 2010, the poverty headcount measure in Indonesia "was higher than any other Southeast Asian country except Laos" (Booth 2016, 193). One reason for the high poverty figures in 2010 was because, starting in 2004, rice prices spiked on the international market; and with tight restrictions on imports, domestic prices stayed above elevated world prices. As a result, millions of low-income Indonesians suffered further hardship. It is estimated that the poor spend one-third of their income on food. This includes the urban and rural poor; even most rice farmers remain net consumers of rice. In addition to the state importer (Bulog), smugglers, and rice millers, higher rice prices benefited larger, land-owning farmers who could produce a surplus for the domestic market. Indonesian officials protested profusely against the findings of the World Bank that the government's own pricing policy worsened poverty (McCulloch 2008).

It is in this comparative and contested context that the macroeconomic performance under Yudhoyono was lamented as a series of "missed opportunities" (Hill 2015, 289). One problem has been that Indonesia's growth rates of 5.5 percent are achieved easily. Prominent attributes of the country's economy almost naturally lend themselves to some magnitude of growth – fiscal discipline, a mammoth domestic market, a vast reservoir of natural resources, semi-open trade policies, a young and passably educated population, a favorable geographic position located in a high-growth region, and a legacy of New Order economic technocracy that is committed to a modicum of export-oriented manufacturing. At times, these elements can be a blessing, as demonstrated during the 2008 global financial downturn when Indonesia weathered the crisis better than many of its neighbors. Their more open and globally integrated economies left them exposed to the contraction in international trade (Basri 2015). Yet, when the world economy is not in crisis, which is more often

---

[35] Growth rates have been taken from the World Bank (http://data.worldbank.org/indicator/NY .GDP.MKTP.KD.ZG).

[36] These figures have been take from www.indonesia-investments.com/news/news-columns/pov erty-rate-indonesia-11.1-of-population-in-september-2015/item6341?.

than not, Indonesia's moderate growth rates lull policymakers and politicians, such as Yudhoyono, into complacency and depress their incentives to fight the necessary political battles to introduce further reforms that are required to achieve higher growth. Worse, these rates are used by opponents of liberalization to roll back whatever market reforms have been made, which means more growth-retarding protectionism and overbearing state involvement in the economy (Patunru & Rahardja 2015). Finally, the ease with which Indonesia now achieves growth does not hide the fact that the government lacks the institutional capabilities to induce the technological upgrading, most critically in the education sector, to break out of the hotly contested middle-income trap (Coxhead & Li 2008).[37]

More than any other factor, it was the commodity boom of 2005–11 that bolstered the Indonesian economy but at the same time suppressed Yudhoyono's urgency to initiate or institute economic reforms. It is estimated that the sharp increases in the prices of such prime export commodities as nickel, coal, and palm oil alone added between 1 and 1.5 percent to Indonesia's growth figures over this period. In fact, economists noted that the "value of commodity exports more than tripled from 2004 to 2011 and the value of all exports nearly tripled – an increase of $130 billion in seven years" (Papanek, Pardede, & Nazara 2014, 46).

Spurred by high demand from the rising economic powerhouses of China and India, the commodity boom also negatively affected Indonesia's economy and society. For example, fueled by high commodity prices, investors, prospectors, and speculators opened more fields on marginal lands, including peatlands, across Kalimantan, Sumatra, and the Riau islands. Fires deployed to clear land for oil palm but also coal mines caused haze so widespread that in 2015 it enveloped Singapore, Malaysia, and even southern Thailand for weeks (Varkkey 2016). Of course, its effects were felt most acutely by Indonesians living in the vicinity of the burnings. While agribusiness conglomerates and local governments denied responsibility, the World Bank estimated that the haze's disruption of local economies and school systems and the resulting spike in public health emergencies cost some US$16 billion (Alisjahbana & Busch 2017; Purnomo et al. 2017).

Another detrimental effect of the commodity boom was the decline of the manufacturing sector's contribution to the national economy, which fell from 28 percent in 2004 to 21 percent by 2014.[38] In part, manufacturing's slump was caused by an influx of foreign direct investment into the natural-resource

---

[37] Contrarily, Rock does not believe Indonesia is inhibited by the middle-income trap (2017, chapter 7).

[38] These figures are taken from www.theglobaleconomy.com/Indonesia/Share_of_manufacturing/.

extraction sector. This in turn led to the appreciation of the Indonesian rupiah, which made the country's manufactured exports more expensive internationally (while it brought higher profits for sought-after export commodities). For many economists, labor's growing political influence (on account of competitive elections) also contributed to manufacturing's decline.[39] The increase in inflexible policies with respect to wage readjustments and retrenchment led to a loss in regional competitiveness. These same economists warned that employment opportunities in turn would be threatened in the medium-to-long term (Manning & Roesad 2007; Aswichahyono, Hill, & Narjoko 2010).

Lastly, Indonesia's crumbling infrastructure – unreliable electricity, inefficient port facilities, jammed expressways – depressed manufacturing's capacity. Owing to the financial crisis, Indonesia's tight financial position delayed upgrades in infrastructure for nearly six years. But by 2004, the economy had recovered to a point where such investments were becoming feasible (World Bank 2004). Yudhoyono seemed intent on drumming up investment demand by hosting a lavish Infrastructure Summit ninety days into his first administration. The president had bought into the concept of the public–private partnership to finance projects. Promoted by multilateral organizations, public–private partnerships, in theory, promise private investors special benefits and cost advantages. In return, the government gets infrastructure projects developed with a lower burden on its own finances. But bureaucratic red-tape, flimsy property rights protections, an immature domestic bond market, and the inability of a weakened central government to enforce its eminent domain powers in order to appropriate land in a timely fashion deterred many investors (foreign and domestic alike) from committing their millions to project development.[40] Damningly, Yudhoyono's administrations were also unwilling to spend the public monies necessary even in public–private partnership projects; in other words, they sought to pass too much risk onto a reluctant private sector. Instead, beholden to coalition partners, and despite pressure applied by the international financial institutions, Yudhoyono frittered away billions of dollars of public funds each year on fuel subsidies that mostly benefited society's upper-middle class and the rich. Meanwhile, because of price differentials, artificially cheap oil was smuggled out of the country to neighboring countries in enormous quantities. To the surprise of few,

---

[39] On labor's growing prominence, see Caraway and Ford (2014).

[40] For compulsory land acquisition, the central government could no longer rely on the army to "clear" the land, as was common practice during the New Order.

Yudhoyono's 2005 Infrastructure Summit flopped. By mid-2014, at the end of Yudhoyono's second term, not one of the thirty-eight planned tollways had been completed (Davidson 2015a).

From a macro-performance perspective, one problem was that the natural-resource extraction sector added few jobs relative to its expansion. Coupled with manufacturing's slide, millions of young, job-market entrants each year were unable to find employment or were forced into the informal sector or other low-productivity areas such as food-crop agriculture (especially rice farming on Java's notoriously micro-sized plots). This debilitating phenomenon, known as "jobless growth" (Saich et al. 2010), has not only contributed to the decoupling of growth from human development; it has worsened Indonesia's inequality (Rigg 2016, chapter 2; World Bank 2016). Indonesia's Gini coefficient – the standard index that measures a country's income inequality – worryingly rose from 0.38 in 2005 to 0.41 in 2013, or a level "of inequality more typically associated with Latin American than Asian countries" (Papanek, Pardede & Nazara 2014, 45). During the commodity boom, the real consumption of Indonesia's top 20 percent grew by 40 percent, while the bottom 40 percent increased only 17 percent (Papanek, Pardede, & Nazara 2014, 33, chart 7).

In response, and owing to plentiful state coffers on account of the commodity boom, Yudhoyono's first administration did implement expensive new programs aimed at alleviating poverty and delivering health insurance to the poor (rather than a program of job creation).[41] Moreover, Yudhoyono's government ramped up another program that had begun under Megawati to provide special subsidized rice to millions of low-income families across the archipelago. The project was also a convenient way to restore confidence in (or pass rents to) Bulog after its wings were clipped by the IMF during the 1997/8 financial crisis. Unfortunately, almost a fifth of the rice distributed "disappeared" before reaching the program's intended targets (Olken 2006).

Finally, worse than stagnation, economic governance reform efforts suffered setbacks under Yudhoyono. For example, he stood by as members of his ruling coalition – in particular Golkar, headed by Aburizal Bakrie, once Indonesia's richest businessman – relentlessly attacked his Finance Minister, Sri Mulyani

---

[41] Implementation was mostly the domain of local governments, where acute electoral competition motivated local officials to cover millions of low-income Indonesians to an extent that surpassed initial expectations. This rather positive (and surprising) outcome of the interplay among local elections, decentralization, and social security provision has drawn ample scholarly attention to the matter (Rosser 2012; Aspinall 2014b; Fossati 2016, 2017; Pisani, Kok, & Nugroho 2017).

Indrawati, over a botched government takeover of a bank. Indrawati was a bright, hard-nosed reformist technocrat with little patience for the collusion and cronyism characteristic of government–business relations in Indonesia. With little political support and a tarnished image, Indrawati resigned her post in 2010 and left for an executive position at the World Bank in Washington DC.

Yudhoyono's parliamentary allies were also instrumental in disbanding the new Upstream Oil and Gas Regulatory Agency. The establishment of independent regulatory agencies was a prominent part of the program to restructure the institutional governance of the economy. As was covered earlier, a series of liberalizing laws had laid the legal groundwork for these specialized bodies to form. They are consistent with the type of regulatory capitalism that the IMF and World Bank have been trying to impose on Indonesia. In theory, these agencies depoliticize economic governance because they are headed and staffed by nonelected, apolitical technocrats rather than politicians or political appointees. In so-called difficult environments where rule-of-law institutions are weak or compromised, independent regulatory agencies are conceived as mechanisms to help instill a rule-based "good governance" program that enhances accountability, transparency, and predictability in economic policy-making (Davidson 2015a).

Power and predatory interests, however, have overwhelmed the governance outcomes of the new regulatory bodies. Notably, the Upstream Oil and Gas Regulatory Agency had assumed regulatory duties from the notoriously corrupt state oil company, Pertamina. But as the new agency gained operational autonomy, vested interests feared that the sector's lucrative resources once available to them were being shuttered. So these interests began to attack the new agency, in particular accusing it of slavishly favoring foreign oil companies. In 2012, riding a wave of resource nationalism, a coalition of Islamic social organizations that meld religious belief with social activism and politics, including Muhammadiyah and Nahdlatul Ulama, filed a case at the Constitutional Court to test the body's constitutionality (Habir 2013). The court ruled that the Upstream Oil and Gas Regulatory Agency unduly interfered with the state's direct control of the country's resources, thereby violating the Economic Democracy Clause of the 1945 Constitution. Its sudden closure forced Yudhoyono to form a temporary agency in order to safeguard the legal certainty of some 300 contracts with an investment value of tens of billions of dollars. This time, the regulatory agency's successor was "safely" tucked under the authority of the Ministry of Energy and Mineral Resources. (Not coincidentally, Yudhoyono once headed this ministry). Almost immediately, the successor agency became embroiled in a corruption scandal (Davidson 2015b).

### 3.3 Identity-based Mobilizations

The success of Islamic activists in the Upstream Oil and Gas Regulatory Agency case showed two things. First, it was becoming increasingly hard to disentangle the identity-based claims of such movements from claims over material resources. Second, the burgeoning of Islamic religiosity in the social-cultural realm introduced in Section 2.3.1 was gaining traction in the arenas of formal politics and political economy.

The 2012 Constitutional Court victory, which expressed a distinct form of Islamic populism, built upon prior accomplishments (Hadiz 2016). In 2003, parliament had passed a controversial law on education that mandated the teaching of Islam to Muslim students even enrolled in private Catholic or Christian schools. In 2005, the Indonesian Council of Islamic Scholars (Majelis Ulama Indonesia, MUI) – an official body sponsored by the New Order but one that has tried to assert its autonomy and authority after Soeharto's abdication – issued a religious ruling (*fatwa*) denouncing secularism, pluralism, and liberalism (Kersten 2015). And after years of heated debate, in 2008, parliament pushed through another contentious law outlawing public displays or activities that were deemed to be "porno-actions." Another instance of Yudhoyono pandering to coalition partners, this act's passing sparked backlash among some ethnic groups, such as the Balinese and West Papuans, who argued that the legislation was an attack on such bedrock features of their culture as dances and clothing (Allen 2007; T. Jones 2013). Although the implementation of the antipornography law on the ground has been patchy at best, like much other legislation in Indonesia, symbolically the promulgation of this particular statute spoke volumes.

More disturbingly, physical attacks against religious minorities accompanied these legislative victories, casting a cloud over Yudhoyono's putative desire for moderation and stability (McBeth 2016). Especially in Jakarta's suburbs, churches became frequent targets of politically motivated vandalism. Defenders of these provocations claimed the churches lacked proper zoning permits, to which the congregations retorted that such licenses were never forthcoming from local officials (Crouch 2014). Violence against a heterodox, Islamic sect known as Ahmadiyah also rose. The government banned proselytization by the sect in 2008. Afraid of alienating chief coalition partners and his support base, Yudhoyono fueled the escalation through inaction (Platzdasch 2013; Menchik 2014).

Lesbian, gay, bisexual, and transgender (LBGT) individuals and groups were also targeted. There has been a pointed debate in Indonesia over the degree of tolerance or marginalization of LGBT communities historically – for example, when and why such terms as *gay* and *lesbi* entered the Indonesian lexicon as social categories, and how different class positions have influenced self-identification with or stigmatization of certain labels (Oetomo 1996; Boellstorff 2005). Still, in post-Soeharto Indonesia, not unlike other civil society organizations, these groups had taken advantage of the period's broadening civil liberties and freedoms. But as their LBGT-themed confer-ences and related publications grew in number, these developments elicited sporadic and uncoordinated attacks. The attacks, along with occasional outbursts of public condemnation, were serious enough to prompt anthro-pologist Tom Boellstorff (2007) to warn (presciently) of the possibility of "political homophobia" taking hold.

Recriminations against the country's minority Shi'a community were also troubling (Human Rights Watch 2013). Here, the central government cravenly hid behind the guise of decentralization, arguing that most such disturbances were local matters for local governments to handle (Brown n. d.). The dynamics of decentralization and competitive elections contributed to the passing of *shari`a*-inspired local regulations by regional assemblies that threatened the rights of minorities (Salim 2008). Interestingly, nation-alist and not Islamic or Islamist political parties were responsible for the upturn in such regulations in order to reinforce their religious credentials for electoral purposes (Buehler 2016). This trend amplified the thesis of reli-gious cooptation by nationalist (and formerly secular) political parties in the fierce marketplace for votes (Tanuwidjaja 2010).

During Yudhoyono's time in office, some maintained that puritanical Islam (or, more specifically, Wahhabism) as an educational project had reached its limit in Indonesia. Its advocates, for example, were forced to deviate from the ideology's strict adherence to homogeneity by adapting teachings to local contexts in order to attract students beyond the rural underprivileged (Hassan 2010). Moreover, the ultra-conservative MUI failed to impose its ideological orthodoxy onto its regional counterparts that were enmeshed in messy local political and social contexts (Millie & Hindasah 2015). Many Muslims also were more interested in reconfiguring their faith in order to accommodate rather than reject the challenges and allures of modern capitalism and globa-lization (Rudnyckyj 2010). Meanwhile, a number of Islamic organizations that promote liberal democracy and pluralism continued to advocate their ideals assertively (van Bruinessen 2013b; Kersten 2015). Nevertheless, it was clear to see that Indonesia's famed reputation for tolerance of and respect for religious pluralism was being gravely tested, especially by the nonviolent radical ideology espoused by such fast-growing and influential hardline groups as the Indonesian Hizbut Tahrir (HTI) (S. Jones 2013; Lindsey &

Pausacker 2016). If historian Merle Ricklefs (2012) could characterize Indonesia's twentieth century as a pitched battle between the opponents and proponents of Islamization, the latter were gaining ground as the new century progressed. Indonesian society and politics was heading toward a polarization that will be the subject of the next section.

Before turning to that section, however, some words must be said about the waning of the violent, identity-based mobilizations in the outer islands that had marred the transition's early phase. Like the Islamist movement, these groups too began translating identity claims into material gains. In part, the central government's tactic of allowing the administrative proliferation of regional governments so that a particular religious or ethnic group could dominate its own territory worked (Section 2.1). But as the massive violent conflicts waned, Yudhoyono's administration placed an unofficial moratorium (2009–12) on the local government splitting process because the number of requests was overwhelming the central government bureaucracy.[42] Officials were also displeased with the building of local white elephant projects fueled by the commodity boom and with the political and administrative recalcitrance shown by some district heads (*bupati*). The moratorium was not the only means through which the central government under Yudhoyono was trying to recentralize authority. A 2011 law gave more powers to governors, who paradoxically remain – despite their now elected status – official representatives of the central government (Tomsa 2015). And a 2012 eminent domain law replaced district governments with the National Land Authority to lead the involuntary land appropriation process for development projects in the so-called public interest (Davidson 2015a).

Returning to conflict-reducing mechanisms, another tactic also proved effective – the mixing of candidate tickets in the local elections of governors, mayors, or district heads. After the direct election for the presidency was adopted in 2004, it became inevitable that the process would be expanded to the regions (Erb & Sulistiyanto 2009). As a result, local mafias, and to a lesser extent party machines, proliferated (Tans 2012). There was some violence related to these new elections, especially against the offices of local parties and local electoral commissions. Yet, particularly in ethnically mixed districts with a history of conflict, local elites over time learned that interethnic cooperation pays (Tadjoeddin 2014).[43] Most districts remain financially dependent on central government block grants, and the central government can simply

---

[42] Small-scale, violent incidents, however, persisted, especially in new districts with poor records of service delivery (Barron, Jaffrey, & Varshney 2016; Pierskalla & Sacks 2017).

[43] A new disturbing tactic seems to be the intimidation of opposition candidates (Harish & Toha n.d.).

turn off the resource tap to warring sides (or delay the transfer of legally mandated funds) (Lewis 2014). So, alongside political party considerations, candidate tickets now often showcase representatives from different identity groups. Depending on the locale, a Protestant might pair with a Muslim in formerly violence-stricken Poso, for instance (Brown & Diprose 2009); in West Kalimantan, a Chinese might pair with a Dayak or a Malay to ensure multiple elite interests remain satisfied. As district elections became more competitive, but also more ethnically homogenous (due to district splitting), violence over local electoral outcomes subsided because winning coalitions have needed to rely on minority voters (Toha 2017). Overall, given that there have been more than a thousand local elections held in democratic Indonesia, and given the thuggery that can surround electoral politics (Wilson 2015), remarkably few people have died in connection with local direct elections – save perhaps most worryingly in West Papua (Nolan, Jones, & Solahudin 2014). Certainly, a wide distribution of electoral spoils among local party elites, contractors, business-men, retired or active military officials, and local gangsters helped to condition this outcome. These networks blurred distinctions between legal and illegal activities and the boundaries between state and society (Aspinall & van Klinken 2010).

Lastly, as interests of the *adat* movement began to intersect with that of party politics in local elections, it led to the question of whether Indonesia had become a deeply ethnicized polity, like its neighbor Malaysia. Some disagreed (Aspinall 2011). One mitigating factor involved the ban on local or ethnic-based parties (save for Aceh) (Horowitz 2013). Another factor, however, was more disturbing: that communal violence and district proliferation led to more ethnically homogenous local governments and societal segregation (Adam 2010; Toha 2017; Colombijn 2018).

In all, the degree to which ethnicity defines local political society varies widely across Indonesia. Ethnicity as an influence will continue for the foreseeable future, as the local and national-level lobbying efforts of the *adat* movement for legal recognition of traditional claims over resources and other governance matters has scored some victories (Bedner & van Huis 2008).[44] Strides made in some realms have spilled into others. Notable has been the regularity with which political parties and candidates for office promote ethnic symbols in campaigns when local context dictates (Fox 2018). The electoral-related politicization of ethnicity and religion in the

---

[44] In this struggle the Constitutional Court's 2012 decision (issued in 2013) to recognize the resource rights of indigenous peoples has been a milestone; key ministerial regulations subsequently have since been issued (Fay & Denduangrudee 2016).

outer islands eventually and disturbingly made its way to Jakarta, leading to intense national political uproar. This furor will feature in the following section.

## 4 Polarization

The rapid ascent of Joko Widodo – popularly known as Jokowi – took Indonesia by storm. His rise from mayor of a medium-sized city in Central Java to the presidency in a matter of years sparked a debate on whether this development represented a victory for democratic pluralism (Ford & Pepinsky 2014). A true outsider, Jokowi lacked ties to the New Order. But evidence also mounted that Jokowi the reformer would not be able to clean up Indonesian politics by himself, or even that in the end he wanted to do so. After all, the large parties made sure that Jokowi's climb took place within the confines of party politics and their patronage networks. Meanwhile, vote-buying during the 2014 legislative elections reached unprecedented heights, and retired generals other than Yudhoyono revived their power considerably. The most graphic example is Prabowo Subianto, who lost the presidential race to Jokowi in 2014. Having led a brutal military campaign in East Timor, and responsible for the disappearance of about two dozen democracy activists toward the end of Soeharto's rule, Prabowo most viscerally represents the coercive legacies of the New Order.

As president, and in response to decentralization and an empowered parliament – or put differently, a dispersal of political authority – Jokowi is amassing immense resources under his command by building up the state sector, especially in the form of public enterprises. This growth of state capitalism reduces the access of the country's rent-seeking private sector to state resources; it also further marginalizes the mix of regulatory and market capitalism that the IMF has promoted. Coupled with an infusion of foreign investment from the Northeast Asian rivals of Japan and China, state-led development is the primary means through which Jokowi is seeking to massively upgrade the country's dilapidated infrastructure in a postcommodity boom economy. In contrast to Yudhoyono, Jokowi is becoming the "Infrastructure President." Whether gains from his investment program will trickle down to the society's neediest remains to be seen.

The period's most pitched political battle, however, took place over Jakarta's governorship in late 2016 and early 2017; the contestation prompted the largest and most violent rallies in the nation's capital since Soeharto's 1998 downfall. Demonstrations and the subsequent election announced to the world that political Islam had indeed arrived on Indonesia's national stage. No longer marginal or marginalized, this movement is increasingly infiltrating and defining Islam's mainstream. But it is also fostering an environment of intolerance that threatens religious and other minorities, while wrenching open searing fissures over national identity and citizenship. There is concern over the diminishing roles that civility, democratic pluralism, and diversity play in politics and society. Regrettably, a pressured Jokowi is fighting back by turning to repressive measures that recall New Order practice. Presently, polarization is Indonesia's defining political feature.

## 4.1 Politics

The large political parties succeeded in limiting participants for the 2014 legislative election to only twelve parties. Tougher national party eligibility requirements squashed the aspirations of smaller hopefuls. A permanent branch office was needed in every province, in three-quarters of the municipalities/districts in every province, and in half of those municipalities/districts. Existing parties also raised the parliamentary electoral threshold to 3.5 percent, which denied seats to the two last-place finishers in the balloting.[45] The two big movers took advantage of the Democrat Party's precipitous fall. PDI-P's popular vote total improved from 14 to 19 percent for the 2014 election, making it parliament's top party. And Prabowo's Great Indonesia Movement Party (Partai Gerakan Indonesia Raya or Gerindra) jumped from eighth to third by bagging 12 percent of the vote. Golkar's vote tally (about 14 percent) and parliamentary seat allocation (second largest) held steady from 2009.

The 2014 contest also brought an unwanted development for the parties – a surge in vote-buying. Blame for this acute uptick cannot be solely pinned on party machinations, for it resulted from the Constitutional Court's 2008 decision to declare closed party lists unconstitutional. These are where voters choose a party on the ballot and party leadership decides who is awarded a parliamentary seat; the closed list was practiced under the New Order.[46] Because open lists with visible candidate names loosen party-elite control over their candidates, it contributes to more individual-oriented campaigns, increased intraparty competition, and ultimately higher levels of vote-buying (Kunicová & Rose-Ackerman 2005).

---

[45] Exceptions included three Aceh-based parties contesting elections only in Aceh. That local parties are allowed in this formerly restive province was a major component of the peace accord.

[46] In this way, the Constitutional Court's contribution to democracy has been mixed. That judges were viewed with having a high degree of professionalism lent legitimacy to their decisions on dozens of disputes over national and especially regional electoral outcomes (Mietzner 2010), until 2013 when a corruption scandal over the adjudication of local electoral cases tarnished the court's reputation, unfortunately including those of its honest judges.

The effect of the 2008 decision was not fully realized until the 2014 contest. Campaigning in Indonesia had been evolving. Defining practices included forming success teams, hiring polling and survey firms, and paying for increasingly expensive television advertisements. But these trends pertained to national-level races (or in regions of relative wealth) (Qodari 2010). The vote-buying in the 2014 legislative elections, however, reached new heights. Conducted by old and newer parties alike, practices across the country involved cash payments to individuals and the provision of club goods (commodities that only a certain group of voters can enjoy, such as targeted health care, a football field, or mechanized farming equipment) (Aspinall & Sukmajati 2016). As in Thailand and the Philippines, reliance on vote canvassers – those who are paid to corral voters or provide block votes – is now pervasive. Equally pervasive are candidates worried that they cannot trust brokers to deliver what they have been paid to do (Aspinall 2014a). This explosion in vote-buying represents an extreme example of the theme of the decentralization of corruption that has prominently figured in debates of post-Soeharto politics and political economy. In 2014, the vote-buying was so widespread that scarcely any party gained an advantage from the practice. But to individual politicians who competed against each other within the same party, the penalty for not engaging in it was severe: not being elected. Signs suggest vote-buying will be as extensive (if not more so) in the 2019 elections.

It is remarkable, then, that the subsequent 2014 presidential race tested Indonesia's young electoral democracy more profoundly. The caustic campaign arguably demonstrated the tepid commitment of the Indonesian elite and electorate to the concept and practice of competitive elections. During his campaign for the presidency, the controversial Prabowo repeatedly attacked democracy for being incompatible with so-called Indonesian culture. His harsh words and his popularity heightened concern about a possible slide toward authoritarianism. Championing a martial and Islamic image of Indonesia, the formal general with a deplorable human rights record openly discussed discontinuing direct executive elections and returning to the country's original, executive-centric 1945 Constitution.

To the relief of the West, and obviously a majority of Indonesian voters, the ultranationalist Prabowo did not win the election. Yet, having a candidate who had brazenly called for the dismantling of the country's democracy to receive nearly 47 percent of the vote produced the specter – the real possibility, even – of reversing the hard-won gains of the years of democratic rule, in particular institutionalized competitive multiparty elections and civil liberties. It suggested that a far greater number of Indonesians than most suspected were dissatisfied with Western-style democracy; indeed, that they appeared to desire a return to a coercive and violent past (Mietzner 2014b).

At the same time, institutionally and symbolically, Jokowi's victory marked a milestone for Indonesia's democracy. Institutionally, because Indonesia technically passed Samuel Huntington's famous two-turnover test of democratic resiliency: "The party or group that takes power in the initial election at the time of transition loses a subsequent election and turns over power to those election winners, and if those election winners then peacefully turn over power to the winners of a later election" (Huntington 1991, 267). When this transpires, says Huntington, democracy can be considered consolidated. It is sufficiently stabilized and institutionalized to make recurrence of dictatorship unlikely, and that chief stakeholders have come to see (peaceful) multiparty elections as the only mechanism for transferring power lawfully. The two-turnover test has been criticized, however, for being top-down and elitist, and for allowing some dubious cases, such as Iraq in recent years, to qualify as stable democracies. Whether Indonesia's electoral democracy can be considered consolidated with Jokowi's victory is debatable. Some rightly worry that either deeply embedded patron–client networks or great wealth imbalances impede the liberal ideal of equality regardless of electoral turnover (Webber 2006; Winters 2011). I once wrote that the unreliability of state officials to implement or be held accountable to the country's laws would keep Indonesia's democracy from being sufficiently consolidated (Davidson 2009). Nothing that has transpired since then has made me change my view. Still, Jokowi's victory did hold symbolic meaning: he was the first post-Soeharto president to be a political product entirely of the reform era.

Jokowi's popularity was forged by two prime tenets of post-Soeharto Indonesia: democracy (local direct elections) and decentralization (the space afforded to implement innovative policies). Neither a former general nor head of a political party, Jokowi was the first outsider to win the presidency. A former furniture salesman, he began his political career as mayor of Surakarta (also known as Solo), a mid-size city in Central Java. His popular programs for the city's poor, such as free health care, and his (trademark) unannounced inspections created a buzz among democracy reformers and civil society activists (Bunnel et al. 2013). His success caught the attention of the country's party bigwigs. In 2012, he was parachuted into the Jakarta's gubernatorial race and won handily.[47] Upon his victory, the self-proclaimed reformer

---

[47] Because Jakarta is the country's capital and largest city and is administratively demarcated as a special province, its head is a governor, not a mayor.

promised he would finish his term and not seek the presidency. (Jokowi broke his promise, just as former US President Barack Obama had done).

Doubters questioned Jokowi's reformist credentials, whether he truly seeks to reduce corruption, sideline vested interests, and increase transparency and accountability in governance (Winters 2013). By law, Jokowi could have run for the Jakarta governorship as an independent candidate, befitting his reformist, outsider image. (Political parties have ensured that independent candidates are barred from running for the presidency). Perhaps because he needed a campaign war chest, or because he knew he needed the cooperation of the parties in Jakarta's provincial assembly to pass his programs, Jokowi chose to run with Megawati's PDI-P. He even teamed with Prabowo's Gerindra Party in the gubernatorial election by naming Basuki Tjahaha Purnama, known as Ahok, as his running mate. Prabowo's wealthy younger brother has been bankrolling Gerindra (Purdey 2016). Here we can see why Prabowo was irritated when Jokowi broke his pledge not to enter the 2014 presidential election. We also glimpse the power of oligarchic money influencing Indonesia's elections (Winters 2013; Hadiz & Robison 2013).

Secular civil society organizations did actively support Jokowi when he ran for the presidency, and tens of thousands of citizens donated money online to his campaign (Tapsell 2015). President Jokowi's early missteps, however, made it seem that the oligarchy thesis was on to something. When he won the presidency, because he was beholden to the interests of Megawati and PDI-P, Jokowi named several party big shots to key portfolios. He even appointed a Megawati confidant and former general with an appalling human rights record as defense minister. This pressure from PDI-P, coupled with Gerindra's "Red and White" coalition (named for the colors of the Indonesian flag) that controlled nearly two-thirds of parliament, accounted for Jokowi's rocky start.

Exploiting the incoming president's vulnerability, the opposition almost succeeded in doing away with direct elections for regional heads.[48] Over time, Jokowi tightened his grip on policymaking, parliament, and thus the presidency, among others, by intervening in the internal affairs of fractious opposition parties. He successfully convinced those such as Golkar and the United Development Party (PPP) to support his presidency (Mietzner 2016). While the question remains as to whether this polarization in parliament spells an end to the party cartel characteristic of Indonesian politics, the

---

[48] In fact, this occurred with a new parliament (based on the 2014 legislative election) but at the end of Yudhoyono's term, before Jokowi was sworn in as president.

constant attending to power struggles marginalized the progressive aspects of Jokowi's agenda (Warburton 2016). To illustrate, in 2017 an acrimonious debate in parliament ensued over the candidature threshold for the 2019 presidential election. Jokowi's block emerged victorious by maintaining cut-offs at one-fifth of parliamentary seats or one-quarter of the popular vote. Because it wanted more than two candidates to enter the election's first round, the Prabowo-led opposition had sought to abolish the threshold altogether.

## 4.2 Political Economy

As in other developing economies, tension between encouraging the private sector or relying on the state to boost economic growth and development has been a prominent feature in Indonesia's political economy for decades (Robison 1986; Robison & Hadiz 2004). One result of the commodity boom under Yudhoyono, however, was to sideline this debate, at least temporarily, since the strong revenue streams and high capital inflows seemed to lessen the debate's urgency. But as commodity prices receded – prices began winding down in 2011, but they had been so inflated that their profitability, though declining, continued through to the end of Yudhoyono's second term – this debate rose to the surface again during Jokowi and Prabowo's tussle for the presidency. On the campaign trail, Jokowi promised to resurrect Indonesia's crumbling infrastructure, something which Yudhoyono had failed to achieve. When he won the presidency, Jokowi ditched Yudhoyono's favored approach, the public–private partnership, and with commodity prices on the wane, devised a state-driven plan to rejuvenate the postcommodity boom economy in general, and to rebuild the country's physical utilities in particular.

Jokowi took the first step in late 2014 when he boldly slashed billions of US dollars from the government's fuel subsidies bill. The windfall was felt immediately. The 2015 state budget allotted a state capital expenditure fund of about Rp. 290 trillion (US$21.5 billion), approximately 86 percent higher than the Rp. 156 trillion of Yudhoyono's final budget. In the 2016 budget, the figure rose to Rp. 313 trillion, which represented nearly 15 percent of the total budget and 2.8 percent of the country's gross domestic product. In 2010, under Yudhoyono, these figures stood at 8.8 percent and 1.5 percent, respectively (Negara 2016).

Increased spending heightened ambitions. Targets stretched credulity: 5,000 kilometers in railway tracks, 2,600 kilometers in roads, 1,000 kilometers in expressways, forty-nine irrigation dams, twenty-four seaports, and power plants with an accumulative capacity of 35,000 megawatts. To put some of these numbers in perspective, ten years of Yudhoyono's rule produced less than

200 kilometers of expressways, and his second administration added only 7,000 megawatts of electricity to the nation's generating capacity.

Rather than doling out state contracts to the country's conglomerates or continuing with the public–private partnership programs that Yudhoyono had pursued, Jokowi is betting his presidency on the state sector. Eventually, his administration hopes to consolidate the unwieldy, and in part unprofitable, state sector and its many firms into six large divisions: mining, construction, banking, property, food, and toll roads. Jokowi certainly has in mind forming a few gigantic state entities similar to China or a sovereign wealth fund like Khazanah Nasional of Malaysia or Temasek Holdings of Singapore (Kim 2018).

State-owned construction companies are benefiting enormously from Jokowi's infrastructure plans, but so are those in other sectors. Consider Jasa Marga, the state toll-road corporation. Partially consistent with IMF-led governance reforms, Jasa Marga had joined a long list of state entities undergoing partial privatization. The rationale was, among others, to gain a degree of autonomy from government interference. This included pressure to build unprofitable routes without proper compensation, which had happened during the New Order (Davidson 2015a).

Following its partial privatization, Jasa Marga's leadership tested its new autonomy. Under Yudhoyono's administrations, they passed on two major government projects with questionable profitability. But Jokowi combined his arm-twisting with sweetening of the proverbial pot to convince Jasa Marga's management to toe his government's line more firmly. The result was a raft of licenses obtained by Jasa Marga in exchange for favorable concessions, low-interest loans from state banks, and lengthy concessionary control (more than forty years in some cases) (Davidson n.d.). It is no wonder, then, that the private sector, represented by the rent-seeking Indonesian Chamber of Commerce, publically voiced its concern over exclusion from Jokowi's infrastructure boom.

Alongside crowding out the private sector, Jokowi's ambitious infrastructure plan has its shortcomings.[49] Whether the program is sufficiently pro-poor counts among them (Warburton 2016). The bulk of Jokowi's massive 35,000 megawatt electricity projects, for example, will be added to the developed islands of Java and Bali where village electrification is more than 95 percent, whereas rates are appallingly low in eastern Indonesia. That these new plants

---

[49] While this may pertain to old style, private sector rent-seeking, it does not foreclose emerging entrepreneurial forces and innovation-oriented growth from bearing fruit. Witness the fantastic rise of the ride hailing startup Go-Jek, founded in 2010, with a market evaluation of some US$3 billion as of early 2018.

will be coal-fired also raises questions about Jokowi's commitment to lowering Indonesia's greenhouse gas emissions, to which previous governments had pledged.

Finance is another limitation. The program's scale, estimated at US$400 billion in order to support economic growth targets of 6–8 percent per annum, outstrips the state's financial capacities. This became clear in 2016 when the state experienced a tax revenue shortfall of almost Rp. 220 trillion on account of low commodity prices. Receipts from a tax amnesty program, instituted by Jokowi's administration in 2016, helped to fill 2017 budgetary gaps. But the original plan had been to use receipts from the tax amnesty program to help finance Jokowi's infrastructure plans. The amnesty included both voluntary repatriation of funds held abroad and penalty payments on unpaid taxes that started low and progressively rose over time. By late 2016, the program had generated about Rp.97.2 trillion (US$7.5 billion) in revenue, falling between the expectations of the central bank (Rp. 53 trillion) and those of the government (Rp. 165 trillion). Nevertheless, weak institutions make it less likely that sorely needed reform of the state's tax administration will produce long-term, sustainable results (Hamilton-Hart & Schulze 2016).

Injections of foreign direct investment are also financing Jokowi's infrastructure ambitions, despite the rousing rhetoric of economic nationalism during the 2014 presidential campaign. After all, Jokowi and Prabowo ardently championed increased economic self-sufficiency, especially in food-crop production (Davidson 2018). Japan has been a longtime investor in Indonesia, and Jokowi as governor sought its help in building a new underground rapid transport system for Jakarta. But the ratcheting up of the rivalry between China and Japan for regional supremacy is playing out on the ground in Indonesia. With the establishment of the Asian Infrastructure Investment Bank in Beijing and the launch of the multibillion One Belt One Road Initiative under President Xi Jinping, China is determined to expand its (soft) power and policy influence throughout Asia (as well as to export its excess capacity in construction and infrastructure). China, the first country Jokowi visited as president, pledged billions in soft loans for infrastructure projects.

Troubles plaguing a high-speed rail link between Jakarta and Bandung, however, are microcosms of the problems that threaten to derail Jokowi's infrastructure ambitions. First, the central government controversially concluded a deal with the state-owned China Railway International after cancelling a prior loan agreement with the Japanese International Cooperation Agency. The former stepped in with a sweeter offer, according to which the project did not require funding from the Indonesian government. The move angered the Japanese government and caused concern among other foreign investors. Balancing the high-stakes competition between these two Northeast Asian powerhouses will require delicate diplomacy. Second, there are questions over the economics of the 142-kilometer railway, since a toll road connecting Jakarta to Bandung was built not so long ago. Third, with Chinese investment come Chinese workers – some with legal permits to work on these infrastructure projects, some without to work elsewhere. Nevertheless, their inflow is not only raising tensions between the two governments, but is also spilling over into increased hostility toward local ethnic Chinese (see Section 4.3).

Lastly, problems related to land acquisition along the proposed route is delaying the Jakarta-to-Bandung railway, teaching Chinese investors that in a democracy, however flawed, people cannot be thrown off their lands as easily as under authoritarian conditions. Similar problems had bedeviled infrastructure projects under Yudhoyono, so much so that in his second term he pushed through parliament a law specifically pertaining to compulsory land acquisition in the public interest (Davidson 2015a).[50] Its effect on the ground thus far has been minimal at best.

In fact, the shift toward state control rather than the growth of a regulated, market-based economy was emergent prior to Jokowi's presidency (see Section 3.2). In 2009, for example, parliament passed two new acts: a replacement of the electricity law and one on mining, both of which were quite state-centric (and thereby anti foreign investor). These were followed by the aforementioned Constitutional Court's decision against the Upstream Oil and Gas Regulatory Authority in 2012. Earlier, we noted the rising force of nationalist, populist, and Islamic reactions against liberalization and the increasing worry among politicians and officials that, with the introduction of direct presidential elections and rising campaign costs, their access to these lucrative sectors was being constrained by the new neoliberal governance arrangements (Habir 2013; Hadiz 2016; Davidson 2016). These developments also help to explain the recent mounting of pressure on the American mining giant, Freeport McMoran, to divest its shares from the massive Grasberg mine in West Papua after more than four decades in operation.

These factors are helpful, but they still cannot fully explain Jokowi's dramatic turn toward statism. The example of China's remarkable state-led growth

---

[50] Before this, Soeharto and post-Soeharto presidents had issued presidential decrees and other government regulations.

certainly is influencing Jokowi. We also need to consider Jokowi's statism as a reelection strategy.[51] Jokowi has more control over state firms than he does over private companies, and resources of the former can be used for campaign purposes. Lastly, the shift toward state capitalism aims to strengthen the presidency as an institution in the face of the diffusion of political authority characteristic of the post-Soeharto period. As was mentioned earlier, during the early phases of Indonesia's democratization, the presidency was weakened by design to further democracy and forestall authoritarianism. Decentralization further lessened central government control over recalcitrant regional leaders, many of whom now possess access to resource bases independent of Jakarta. For these reasons and more, the assets of state-owned enterprises – reportedly at US$538.5 billion in 2017 – are nearly eight times higher than they were ten years ago.[52] This is a tremendous treasure chest under the direct control of the central government, and especially that of the president. The question is no longer whether state capitalism is on the ascent in Indonesia, but for how long.

## 4.3 Identity-based Mobilizations

Polarization between state capitalism and private sector capitalism – of either the regulatory or crony variety – is growing acute under Jokowi's presidency, but it has yet to reach the level of polarization that is ensuing in the realm of identity politics. One notable example is the escalation in the frequency and viciousness of attacks against the LGBT community, the state's complicity in the backlash, and the broad societal quiescence, if not tacit consent, of this victimization. The other is rising tensions between the socio-political forces of conservative Islam and proponents of pluralism and a secular state.

During the first year or so of Jokowi's presidency, anti-LGBT harassment escalated – the police roughed up protesters during LGBT rallies, Muslim militias dispersed public meetings and seminars on LGBT themes, and pressure was applied to Facebook and WhatsApp to delete LGBT-related emojis (Human Rights Watch 2016).[53] Then, in early 2016, following an anti-LGBT headline published by an Islamic newspaper and inflammatory comments from the Education Minister about banning LGBT groups from universities,

---

[51] This is certainly a less relevant matter for China's President Xi Jinping, especially now that he has abolished term limits.

[52] These figures were taken from a leading news magazine (*Tempo*) in Indonesia (https://en.tempo .co/read/news/2017/02/07/056843742/SOE-Assets-to-Grow-11-in-2017; February 7, 2017).

[53] In early 2018, Google bowed to pressure by agreeing to remove LGBT-related apps from its Play Store.

a "floodgate of hostility" was opened up against LGBT communities (Kwok 2016). Puzzlingly, there was no immediate provocation – for instance, a LGBT-led campaign to demand the right to same-sex marriage. Activists had been careful, even conservative, in their advocacy.

The intimidation forced civil society allies to abandon embattled LGBT groups. Worse, such major organizations as Nahdlatul Ulama, perhaps in hopes of wrenching influence from hardline groups that increasingly are coming to dominate mainstream Islam, joined the chorus of condemnation.[54] So too did the once obscure Indonesian Psychiatrists Association, which published statements classifying homosexuality as a mental disorder.

Central government figures either remained disturbingly silent on the controversy (President Jokowi among them), or joined the discrimination (Warburton 2016). The defense minister claimed that the LGBT movement was "part of a proxy war by 'foreign influences' to conquer Indonesia" (Kuddus 2017, 85, note 69). Meanwhile, similar to the example of *shari`a*-inspired regional regulations (Section 3.3), local assemblies passed regulations defining homosexuality behavior as "immoral" (Human Rights Watch 2016). Christian and Hindu groups also jumped on the anti-LGBT bandwagon. Throughout 2017, the police rounded up gay men for supposedly engaging in homosexual activity in Aceh, Jakarta, and elsewhere. And a coalition of conservative groups petitioned the Constitutional Court to ban sex outside marriage, which in effect would have made homosexuality a crime. Although in late 2017 the Court narrowly struck down the petition, with strong political party backing, it is likely that revisions to the country's criminal code will vindicate the conservative coalition's legal crusade.

With Soeharto's political demise, elements within the Indonesian state and those with ties to radical Islam had tried to stoke anticommunist fears within society anew. Having failed, they seemingly turned their attention to LGBT communities, Indonesia's new "bogeymen," who now rank ahead of (or alongside) communists, Jews, and ethnic Chinese as the country's hated groups (Oetomo & Sciortino 2017). When we consider the attacks against religious minorities (Christians, Ahmadis, and Shi'a), Ahok (see later in this subsection), and the LGBT communities together, the future of civil public discourse and attendant liberties in Indonesia looks bleak. The thesis of a dominant, democratic, civil Islam in Indonesia is becoming harder to defend (Hefner 2000).

---

[54] It is equally true that many members of the organization likely hold homophobic views as well.

The increased hostility toward the LGBT community garnered international attention, but this was surpassed by the international focus on the fierce politicking over the governorship of the country's capital, described as a "battle for the nation's soul" (Kurniawati 2017). Political inroads made by conservative Islam and oppositional politics between Prabowo's Red and White Coalition and Jokowi's PDI-P-led block, in late 2016, spilled onto the streets of the country's capital with great emotion and force.

The affair in essence began when Jakarta's vice-governor, Ahok, a Chinese Christian originally from East Belitung off the east coast of Sumatra, became governor when Jokowi won the presidency in 2014. (Recall from Section 3.3 the penchant for mixed ethnic candidacy tickets). In September 2016, Ahok's reelection campaign experienced an unexpected jolt – a video surfaced showing him purportedly demeaning Islam through his own interpretation of a Quranic verse.[55] The video went viral as hateful misinformation and manipulation was unleashed by social media (Lim 2017). Amid rising tensions, a coalition of Islamist groups, which included the Islamic Defenders Front (FPI) and the Indonesian Hizbut Tahrir Party (HTI), organized a large anti-Ahok demonstration in Jakarta on November 4, 2016. Peaceful at first, the protest ended in the capital's worst property violence since May 1998 (reportedly, no ethnic Chinese were killed). To mollify the Islamist coalition leaders, Ahok was subsequently charged with blasphemy. The tactic backfired, because on December 2, 2016, a larger rally of one-half to three-quarters of a million people filled central Jakarta. It was widely believed that besides Prabowo, Yudhoyono contributed financially to the rallies in order to benefit his son who was also a candidate in the gubernatorial election. (His son finished last during the first round of voting; Fealy 2016a.)

During court proceedings, it became obvious that his religion and ethnicity were what was on trial. In the end, the politicized stratagems cost him the election. Although Ahok had received the most votes during the first round, the persistent, coordinated attacks against him caused his vote tally to fall below the 50 percent threshold necessary to prevent a runoff, which he subsequently lost.[56] The victory of his opponent, Anies Baswedan, a former Jokowi cabinet minister, showed how politicians can be rewarded by swaying to the

---

[55] Specifically, Ahok was responding to the use of the Qur'an to enjoin Muslims not to vote for a non-Muslim (*kafir*), and he told them not to be "fooled" by such tactics.

[56] The court sentenced Ahok to a two-year jail term, although state prosecutors following the election's outcome recommended probation. Ahok opted not to appeal the decision. Having spent some nine months in jail, in early 2018 Ahok did file his case with the Supreme Court for review, which was subsequently denied.

temptations of sectarianism. Once known as a pluralist, Anies did an about-face and helped to stoke anti-Ahok sentiments. Meanwhile, Anies's win boosted Prabowo's allies in the key regional elections held in mid-2018 and Prabowo's own chances in the 2019 presidential election.

What does the Ahok affair say about the empowerment of ethnic Chinese in postauthoritarian Indonesia? Bigotry and racism contributed to Ahok's loss, but this reality must be tempered against the political strides members of this minority have made elsewhere. Their presence is now notable in parliament, and especially in local assemblies in areas with sizable ethnic Chinese populations – the provinces of North Sumatra, Riau Archipelago, West Kalimantan, and the municipalities contained therein. Nor did the late 2016 rallies result in a "deadly ethnic riot" (Horowitz 2003) that might have happened during Soeharto's time. Still, the affair revealed what might happen to an economically powerful yet politically marginalized minority that comes too close to acquiring real power. Cleansing Indonesia of its longstanding anti-Chinese proclivities would have required more than an Ahok victory. What the episode did was to bring the generally permissive post-Soeharto era for Indonesia's Chinese communities to a close. Explicit anti-Chinese sentiments returned to prominence in mainstream, Indonesian public discourse.

Nationally, the unprecedented politicization of ethnicity and religion during the Jakarta election sparked public debate about what being a citizen in today's Indonesia means and society's commitment to pluralism and diversity. The stress on institutionalizing democratic reforms from the moment Soeharto resigned twenty years ago gave way to struggles over national identity and the state ideology.

The ideological contestation between conservative, Islamist forces and pluralist counterparts remains readily apparent; pitched contestation of identity politics in the electoral sphere is the new normal. What was once an outer-island phenomenon has "gone national." (Lest we forget, integral to the Ahok affair was the political mechanism that defines local politics – the election of a regional head.) The successful politicization of the blasphemy case showed that conservative Islamist factions have become better funded, organized, and politically connected, and thus capable of mobilizing votes at key elections. Whether these forces can stay united remains to be seen. Historically, political Islam, as we have seen above, has tended to break into factions, especially electorally.

The clarity of this movement's ideology and its internationalist orientation has differed from the defenders of the secular state. This camp, led by President Jokowi, is encouraging its own brand of populism too, although Jokowi's side is struggling to articulate a constructive response to conservative Islam. For example, Jokowi's administration is promoting the state ideology of *Pancasila* as a response; *Pancasila* an ideology, however, was abused and manipulated by the New Order. Jokowi's desperate attempt, which includes a new government task force on the subject, headed by Megawati, illustrates the ideological emptiness of this camp.[57] Grounding a secular ideology in the notion of Indonesian citizenship may have been desirable, until an upsurge in sectarianism (among Muslims *and* Christians) threatened to override conventional notions of what it means to be Indonesian today. The understandings of citizenship in this sprawling, archipelagic nation-state are undergoing historic renegotiation and debate.

The revival of *Pancasila* has been accompanied by an upturn in repression, a tried and tested New Order tactic. For example, Jokowi banned the HTI for its leading role in the anti-Ahok demonstrations, although Jokowi's administration publically stressed that the ban was the result of the group's ideology, which challenged the supposed ideals of *Pancasila* (Arifianto 2017). The ban was facilitated by a new strict law on mass organizations. Similarly, Jokowi targeted the FPI, which has attacked symbols of Western liberalism and other political opponents throughout the post-Soeharto period. (Fearing arrest, its firebrand leader, Rizieq Shihab, fled the country.) Jokowi also resurrected the malodorous practice of applying treason charges against opponents. A retired army general, Megawati's sister, and others were arrested for subversion also in connection with the Jakarta demonstrations (Brown 2017).[58]

Some of these dynamics have to do with Jokowi's unfolding and at times uneasy relationship with the armed forces. He needs military backing for his reelection campaign, and unsurprisingly is placing loyalists in strategic posts. But Jokowi lacks the sway over the institution that Yudhoyono had when he was president. Some elements of the armed forces, worried over Jokowi's rumored leftism, are increasing pressure on the country's marginal leftist movement, for example, cancelling seminars on the army's role in the 1965–6 massacres or those on societal reconciliation (Kuddus 2017; Robinson 2018, 264–91). But Jokowi is not averse to currying favor with the military, even prior to reelection maneuverings. Consider his emphasis on self-sufficiency in food. Even though Indonesia is now the world's largest importer of wheat, public condemnation instead has focused on persistent rice imports as a symbol of foreign food dependency and of the demise of the country's agrarian past. (Indonesia imports anywhere from 1 to 5 percent of its annual domestic rice requirements, which includes consumption and public stockpiling needs). So, by stressing increased production and sourcing

---

[57] For the background to the development of this ideology, see Bourchier (2015).

[58] Even West Papuan protesters in Manado, North Sulawesi in December 2016 were arrested on treason charges (Kammen 2017).

of more food crops domestically, Jokowi is allowing the army to utilize its territorial command system to enhance its local presence by opening new rice fields or by mobilizing villagers to grow more rice. The policy relives New Order practices during its own high-profile Green Revolution of the 1970s and 1980s (Syailendra 2017; Davidson 2018). Improved Jokowi-military relations at the grassroots can pay dividends by cultivating voters for the 2019 presidential election. In all, Jokowi is convinced that his enemies pose genuine threats to Indonesia's democracy (Mietzner 2016). As a result, he staunchly believes that their activities and influence must be curtailed. In this respect, he might not be wrong. Relying on means or practices of despotism in order to "save democracy," however, can produce unwanted consequences, especially in a country with a deeply authoritarian history.

## 5 Conclusion

There are plenty of reasons why Indonesia should not be a democracy. Impediments highlighted in the academic literature are found in abundance in this archipelagic nation-state: extreme ethnic and religious heterogeneity, a Muslim-dominant population, low development (below US$4,000 per capita gross domestic product), rich natural-resource endowment, growing inequality, weak institutionalization of constraints on executive power, and a neighborhood of checkered support for democracy (Thailand, Singapore, Vietnam, Malaysia, even China). Other hurdles are harder to quantify, including heritages of feudalism, colonialism, and authoritarianism.

Certainly, the unmistakable retreat of liberal democracy worldwide does not encourage the ideals of equality and freedom in Indonesia. This retreat does tell us that many Indonesians are not alone in struggling to save democracy from its foes. Polarization is rippling across Southeast Asia. In Malaysia, the United Malays National Organization, once the institutionally entrenched ruling party, has stirred up ethnic and religious sentiments sharply in its bid to maintain parliamentary control, despite its surprising electoral loss in 2018. President Rodrigo Duterte's rise in the Philippines and his brutal war against drugs and other supposed enemies of the state have split Philippine society between those favoring his tough, coercive style of governance and those appalled by his disregard for human rights and other hard-won freedoms. Here, the long shadows of authoritarianism have grown darker. In Thailand, urban-rural polarization has driven the country apart for decades. Of late, the divide has crystallized around conservative monarchical authority and military power buttressed by the support of Bangkok's middle and upper-middle classes, on one side, and rural classes in the north and northeast voting heavily for the Shinawatra family and its redistributive policies, on the other side. Even politically inert Singapore has not been immune. Growing xenophobia has forced the governing People's Action Party to take concrete steps before societal concerns manifest themselves at the polls or even break out into movements beyond the narrow confines of formal electoral channels. In this unique city-state, polarization over immigration has the potential to resemble debates currently riveting the United States and the United Kingdom.

Given the structural impediments and growing polarization noted earlier, it is reasonable to ask: How durable is Indonesia's democracy? How long will it last? Is the end near? If Indonesian democracy collapses under the weight of Islamic nationalism, oligarchic power, or military interests, the academic literature will have seemed prophetic. Too many handicaps had overwhelmed the democratic order: The twenty-plus years of democracy were an aberration in Indonesia's *longue durée*. If we are speculating, it is also possible that, even once lost, Indonesians might very well re-mobilize to bring back democracy – a tale akin to Thailand's erratic swings toward and away from open politics.

Who or which strategic group might bring down Indonesia's democracy? First to consider are the country's oligarchs. If oligarchic power has been reaping disproportionate rewards from Indonesia's weak democracy, as the oligarchic thesis implies – for example, determining electoral outcomes and shaping favorable policy decisions due to its tight grip over the media and control of immense material resources – it seems unlikely that the oligarchs would risk destroying it. They also probably do not hold enough common interests to install a more favorable order. By definition oligarchs are enormously wealthy, but they also have diverse backgrounds, different sources of wealth, and varied political views. If oligarchic power, moreover, was threatened enough to overturn Indonesia's democracy, then this democracy arguably would have been more robust than current evaluations suggest. From a rational viewpoint, the oligarchs should be sufficiently satisfied with the country's democracy as is.

The military warrants similar scrutiny. The institution did not inevitably arrive at its advantageous position in post-Soeharto Indonesia. Rather, this position has been the result of strategic planning and fierce defense of corporate interests. The withdrawal from parliamentary representation and removal of active officers from civilian positions proved expedient. It helped free the military from public condemnation – for example, giving it ample space to move behind the scenes as willful, influential actors. Blame for ongoing human rights abuses in West Papua, among other places, can rest with top civilians in the central government as much as members of the armed forces, if not more so. Furthermore, the military's territorial command system remains intact, as does considerable control over an expansive business network of illegal and legal operations. Former officers remain active in party politics and occasionally secure office, from the presidency down to district chiefs. Evidence suggests that this trend is gaining momentum. Hopefully the military learned from Thailand's experience that staging coups is one thing, but governing a country and growing an economy are other things entirely. Coups typically do not resolve intractable political problems; they delay their resolution. This is why military governments, especially following the Cold War, have not endured. Internal divisions over when to return to the barracks plague such regimes. Like the oligarchs, however, the military's current standing has become too favorable.

Islamic nationalism poses the largest threat to Indonesia's democracy because, unlike oligarchs or generals, its opposition is rooted in firm ideological beliefs. I am not suggesting that Islamists do not crave material resources; they do, as do any other rational political actor. But the movement's core principles reject the ideas and values that underpin competitive elections to determine leadership, state law promulgated by mortals, and the belief in the equality of other religions. Islam is compatible with democracy, Islamism less so.

Indonesia is at a crossroads (Hefner 2018). There are questions that are hard to answer: How much genuine support exists among the country's Muslims, who comprise more than 85 percent of the population, for the establishment of an Islamic state? Does the majority prefer to maintain some tenets of democracy alongside a thickening of the public sphere with Islamically inspired values and morals? Expert opinion tends to believe so, although evidence is inconclusive. According to public opinion surveys, support for an Islamic state has grown (albeit from a low base) (Fealy 2016b). Research could likely specify the mechanisms behind this growth. Delineating how far Islamic conservatism in a secular state could expand publically before impinging on the democratic rights and freedoms of others is also murky. Here "others" not only includes minorities, but also encompasses Muslims uncomfortable with the current trend of creeping conservatism. To move forward, Indonesians must deliberate and decide where this line should be drawn, how thick or thin it should be, and how flexible or contextual are its contours.

Of course, such decisions are not necessarily made consciously; yet, the issue is as profound as the constitutional amendments that brought democracy following Soeharto's 1998 ouster. If the constitutional amendments helped to lay the groundwork for twenty years of democratization, then this national conversation over the public role of Islam might provide a signal guide for the next twenty or more. Unlike the constitutional amendments, however, which were mostly decided upon in Jakarta, this public debate needs to take place across the vast archipelago, in its cities, towns, and villages. All Indonesians have a stake in its resolution. Worryingly for those who believe in the country's democracy, a tight pact among antidemocratic forces – substantial factions of Islamists, oligarchs, and military personnel – might prove too potent a combination to overcome. It would make deliberation redundant.

If we speculate further, could the collusive behavior of political parties, which has suppressed the quality of Indonesia's democracy, paradoxically aid in saving the current order? They certainly would be called upon to collaborate. Recall that even the top parties each scarcely gain 20–25 percent of votes cast in national elections. (Non-Islamist parties together obtained roughly 73 or 84 percent of the vote in the 2014 legislative election, depending on how one categorizes Prabowo's Gerindra Party). If truly secular parties no longer exist in Indonesia, could they coalesce to defend competitive elections in a secular state? The last time the parties faced a similar dilemma of saving the country's democratic order in the late 1950s amid the rise of the Indonesian Communist Party they faltered, surrendering to authoritarian pressures by President Sukarno and the armed forces (Lev 1966). But today's context has changed. Democracy has had more time to make inroads, and democratic governments have proven more stable and capable than those of the past, surprising many. Parties have plenty to lose materially (and morally, of course) by yielding to antidemocratic forces. Decentralization, another decisive component of the country's democracy, has been an effective integrative mechanism. Is it capable of doing for democracy what it has done for integration? Prabowo and his allies have already unsuccessfully tried to scrap local direct elections. Will there be enough will to thwart a second attempt?

How long Indonesia's democratic order endures can obviously not be settled here. But scrutinizing the post-Soeharto period (as this Element has done, and encourages others to do) will prove more fruitful than searching for changes from or continuities with Soeharto's regime. While that era casts shadows, the New Order is not fate. What happens to Indonesia's democracy will likely have more to do with developments and dynamics of the post-Soeharto era. Attempts to understand "whither Indonesia?" would do well to grapple with the core logics, central tensions, and the interlinked changes among politics, political economy, and identity-based mobilizations in post-Soeharto periods. They would look, for example, at how the institutional innovation of the transition period or Yudhoyono-led stagnation bred an environment that gave rise to today's polarization. Polarization is more the product of the fusion of political, economic, and societal developments of Indonesia's democratic order than of the authoritarian one.

If polarization intensifies, it will also be progressively more difficult for future research, quantitative or qualitative, to avoid normative implications. The space in which to conduct normal research will likely shrink. We took note earlier of supply-side obstacles to democracy, but those hindrances are perhaps better conceived as unfavorable factors, not deterministic causes. Demand-side factors count too. Researchers need to dig down to discover the precise sources of Indonesia's democratic resiliency in the face of structural constraints and ideological countermovements.

Finally, if societal grievances over poverty and deprivation, rather than ideology, are driving antidemocratic sentiments, as some think, attending to those grievances would make more sense than resorting to New Order-style repression – at least if one believes in democracy. Just how much growth with widening inequality is Indonesian society willing to accept? How many more politicized social security provisions and conditional cash transfer programs does there have to be before a pro-poor coalition in the name of social justice emerges and demands structural change?[59]

Here two key points stand out. One is the entwinement of lessening poverty and mitigating inequality. The creation of formal sector jobs especially in but not limited to manufacturing is critical. Overemployment in food-crop agriculture and in the informal sector leaves too many Indonesians without a steady stream of sufficient income. And those who have barely escaped poverty still remain vulnerable to sudden price shocks of staple goods and susceptible to medical emergencies that often wipe out hard-earned savings. Vicious cycles for tens of millions of poor and near-poor must be broken. Whether the Indonesian poverty line is drawn at US$2.00, US$3.00, or even US$4.00 per day, these amounts are unconscionable in the early twenty-first century in a country of immense resources. Jokowi's infrastructure program must be measured, therefore, not by the number of ribbon-cuttings over which he (or his successor) presides but by the number of good jobs that the new facilities and downstream investments create. Otherwise, the billions spent in public funds would have been wasted.

Then there is the dire state of Indonesia's rule-of-law institutions: legal reforms have made the least progress. Although partial successes, the new Constitutional Court and the Anti-Corruption Commission are but two institutions. The judicial system in fact comprises courts in dozens of provinces and

---

[59] Even these programs remain grossly underfunded, at least at the national level (Patunru & Respatiadi 2017).

hundreds of districts and has continued forth almost as if regime change had not happened (Hurst 2018). Systemic corruption, inadequate budgets, poor management, low professionalization of lawyers, prosecutors, and judges, slow resolution of cases, and high costs for litigants explain why the system is distrusted by the public and why few people seek to use it. The legal system's unreliability also deters needed private investment. Instead, investors are forced to craft ad-hoc, particularistic arrangements and protections with local power-holders (Hamilton-Hart & Palmer 2017). While this approach to contracts and property rights can prove productive for the brave-hearted, it is clearly a second- or third-best solution. With little legal certainty for the private sector, it is no wonder that Jokowi is building up the state sector to unprecedented heights. Relying on the state sector for growth is politically expedient. It is also depressingly true that elites and other insiders benefit from a dysfunctional legal system and the partial enforcement of contracts and property rights. But at some point there must be structural change in the legal system to produce sustainable and truly equitable growth, at least so that the less well-off can strengthen claims over their own property rights.

An incapacitated rule of law also allows thugs and radicals to intimidate and attack minorities and other political opponents with impunity, as the Ahok affair demonstrated. There is no security for victims. The bankruptcy of state law also explains why outer-island ethnic groups and many Muslims have turned to traditional ways of settling disputes. But these ways are known to systematically discriminate against women, outsiders, and members of identity groups who hold different beliefs. The state has failed them and countless others. If the inadequate protection of *all* minorities is not addressed with requisite conviction and resources, Indonesia's democracy might be imperiled.

# References

## Abbreviations

BIES:      *Bulletin of Indonesian Economic Studies*
BKI:       *Bijdragen tot de Taal-, land-, en Volkenkunde*
CSEAPP:    Cornell Southeast Asia Program Publications
ISEAS:     Institute of Southeast Asian Studies
NUS:       National University of Singapore
SEAR:      *South East Asia Research*

Adam, J. (2010). Post-Conflict Ambon: Forced Migration and the Ethno-Territorial Effects of Customary Tenure. *Development and Change*, 41(3), 401–19.

Alisjahbana, A. S. and J. M. Busch (2017). Forestry, Forest Fires, and Climate Change in Indonesia. *BIES*, 53(2), 111–36.

Allen, N. (2014). From Patronage Machine to Partisan Melee: Subnational Corruption and the Evolution of the Indonesian Party System. *Pacific Affairs*, 81(2), 221–45.

Allen, P. (2007). Challenging Diversity? Indonesia's Anti-Pornography Bill. *Asian Studies Review*, 31(2), 101–15.

Anderson, B. (1983). Old State, New Society: Indonesia's New Order in Comparative Historical Perspective. *Journal of Asian Studies*, 42(3), 477–96.

Anwar, D. F. (2010). The Habibie Presidency: Catapulting Toward Reform. In E. Aspinall & G. Fealy, eds., *Soeharto's New Order and Its Legacy: Essays Honouring Harold Crouch*. Canberra: ANU ePress, pp. 99–118.

Arifianto, A. R. (2017). Banning Hizbut Tahrir Indonesia: Freedom or Security? RSIS Commentary, No. 099/2017, May 18, www.rsis.edu.sg /rsis-publication/rsis/co17099-banning-hizbut-tahrir-indonesia-freedom-or-security/#.WUFG-euGPIU.

Aspinall, E. (2009). *Islam and Nation. Separatist Rebellion in Aceh, Indonesia*, Stanford University Press.

(2010). The Irony of Success. *Journal of Democracy*, 21(2), 20–34.

(2011). Democratization and Ethnic Politics in Indonesia: Nine Theses. *Journal of East Asian Studies*, 11(2), 289–319.

(2013). A Nation in Fragments: Patronage and Neoliberalism in Contemporary Indonesia. *Critical Asian Studies*, 45(1), 27–54.

(2014a). When Brokers Betray: Clientelism, Social Networks, and Electoral Politics in Indonesia. *Critical Asian Studies*, 46(4), 96–110.

(2014b). Health Care and Democratization in Indonesia. *Democratization*, 21(5), 803–23.

Aspinall, E. & Fealy, G., eds. (2003). *Local Power and Politics in Indonesia: Decentralisation & Democratisation*, Singapore: ISEAS.

Aspinall, E., Mietzner, M., & Tomsa, D. (2015). The moderating president: Yudhoyono's decade in power. In E. Aspinall, M. Mietzner, & D. Tomsa, eds. *The Yudhoyono Presidency: Indonesia's Decade of Stability and Stagnation*, Singapore: ISEAS, pp. 1–22.

Aspinall, E. & Sukmajati, M., eds. (2016). *Electoral Dynamics in Indonesia: Money Politics, Patronage and Clientelism at the Grassroots*, Singapore: NUS Press.

Aspinall, E. & van Klinken, G., eds. (2010). *The State and Illegality in Indonesia*, Leiden: KITLV Press.

Aswicahyono, H., Bird, K., & Hill, H. (2009). Making Economic Policy in Weak, Democratic, Post-Crisis States: An Indonesian Case Study. *World Development*, 37(2), 354–70.

Aswicahyono, H., Hill, H., & Narjoko, D. (2010). Industrialisation After a Deep Economic Crisis: Indonesia. *Journal of Development Studies*, 46 (6), 1084–108.

Baker, J. (2015). The Rhizome State: Democratizing Indonesia's Off-Budget Economy. *Critical Asian Studies*, 47(2), 309–36.

Barron, P, Jaffrey, S., & Varshney, A. (2016). When Large Conflicts Subside: The Ebbs and Flows of Violence in Post-Suharto Indonesia. *Journal of East Asian Studies*, 16(2), 191–217.

Barter, S. J. (2014). *Civilian Strategy in Civil War: Insights from Indonesia, Thailand, and the Philippines*, New York: Palgrave MacMillan.

Basri, M. C. (2015). A Tale of Two Crises: Indonesia's Political Economy. In T. J. Pempel & K. Tsunekawa, eds., *Two Crises, Different Outcomes: East Asia and Global Finance*. Ithaca: Cornell University Press, pp. 41–63.

Bedner, A. (2008). Rebuilding the Judiciary in Indonesia: The Special Courts Strategy. *Yuridika*, 23(3), 230–53.

Bedner, A. & van Huis, S. (2008). The Return of the Native in Indonesian Law: Indigenous Communities in Indonesia Legislation. *BKI*, 164 (2/3), 165–93.

Bertrand J. (2004). *Nationalism and Ethnic Conflict in Indonesia*, Cambridge University Press.

Boellstorff, T. (2005). *Gay Archipelago: Sexuality and Nation in Indonesia*, Princeton University Press.

(2007). *A Coincidence of Desire: Anthropology, Queer Studies, Indonesia*, Durham: Duke University Press.

Booth, A. (2011). Splitting, Splitting, and Splitting Again: A Brief History of the Development of Regional Government in Indonesia since Independence. *BKI*, 167(1), 31–59.

(2016). *Economic Change in Modern Indonesia: Colonial and Post-colonial Comparisons*, Cambridge University Press.

Borsuk, R. & Chng, N. (2014). *Liem Siong Liong's Salim Group: The Business Pillar of Suharto's Indonesia*, Singapore: ISEAS.

Bourchier, D. (2015). *Illiberal Democracy in Indonesia: The Ideology of the Family State*, London: Routledge.

Bräuchler, B., ed. (2009). *Reconciling Indonesia: Grassroots Agency for Peace*, New York: Routledge.

(2017). Changing Patterns of Mobility, Citizenship and Conflict in Indonesia. *Social Identities*, 23(4), 446–61.

Breman, J. (2001). The Impact of the Asian Economic Crisis on Work and Welfare in Village Java. *Journal of Agrarian Change*, 1(2), 242–82.

Brown, G. (2017). Makar and the re-emergence of old power in Indonesia. *East Asia Forum*, July 30, www.eastasiaforum.org/2017/07/30/makar-and-the-re-emergence-of-old-power-in-indonesia/?utm_source=newsletter&utm_medium=email&utm_campaign=newsletter2017-07-30.

(n.d.). Decentralization, Offloading, and the Regionalisation of Religious Pluralism in Indonesia. Singapore: Asia Research Institute, NUS, unpublished manuscript.

Brown, G. & Diprose, R. (2009). Bare-Chested Politics in Central Sulawesi: The Dynamics of Local Elections in a Post-Conflict Region. In M. Erb & P. Sulistiyanto, eds., *Deepening Democracy in Indonesia? Direct Elections for Local Leaders (Pilkada)*. Singapore: ISEAS, pp. 352–73.

Bubalo, A. & Fealy, G. (2005). Joining the Caravan? The Middle East, Islamism and Indonesia. March. Sydney: Lowy Institute for International Policy, www.lowyinstitute.org/publications/joining-caravan-middle-east-islamism-and-indonesia.

Budianta, M. (2007). The Dragon Dance: Shifting Meanings of Chineseness in Indonesia. In K. Robinson, ed., *Asian Pacific Cosmopolitans: Self and Subject in Motion*. Basingstoke: Palgrave MacMillan, pp. 169–89.

Buehler, M. (2013). Revisiting the Inclusion-Moderation Thesis in the Context of Decentralized Institutions: The Behavior of Indonesia's Prosperous Justice Party in National and Local Politics. *Party Politics*, 19(2), 210–9.

(2016). *The Politics of Shari'a Law: Islamist Activists and the State in Democratizing Indonesia*, Cambridge University Press.

Bunnell, T., Miller, M. A., Phelps, N. A., & Taylor, J. (2013). Urban Development in a Decentralized Indonesia: Two Success Stories? *Pacific Affairs*, 86(4), 857–76.

Bünte, M. (2009). Indonesia's Protracted Decentralization: Contested Reforms and Their Unintended Consequences. In M. Bünte & A. Ufen, eds., *Democratization in Post-Suharto Indonesia*. New York: Routledge, pp. 102–23.

Butt, S. (2007). The Constitutional Court's Decision in the Dispute between the Supreme Court and the Judicial Commission: Banishing Judicial Accountability? In R. H. McLeod & A. MacIntyre, eds., *Indonesia: Democracy and the Promise of Good Governance*. Singapore: ISEAS, pp. 178–99.

(2015). The Rule of Law and Anticorruption Reforms under Yudhyono: The Rise of the KPK and the Constitutional Court. In E. Aspinall, M. Mietzner, & D. Tomsa, eds., *The Yudhoyono Presidency: Indonesia's Decade of Stability and Stagnation*. Singapore: ISEAS, pp. 175–95.

Butt, S. & Lindsey, T. (2008). Economic Reform When the Constitution Matters: Indonesia's Constitutional Court and Article 33. *BIES*, 44(2), 239–62.

Caraway, T. & Ford, M. (2014). Labor and Politics under Oligarchy. In M. Ford & T. B. Pepinsky, eds., *Beyond Oligarchy? Wealth, Power, and Contemporary Indonesian Politics*. Ithaca: CSEAPP, pp. 139–56.

Carney, R. W. & Hamilton-Hart, N. (2015). What Do Changes in Corporate Ownership in Indonesia Tell Us? *BIES*, 51(1), 123–45.

Casson, A. & Obidzinski, K. (2002). From New Order to Regional Autonomy: Shifting Dynamics of "Illegal Logging" in Kalimantan, Indonesia. *World Development*, 30(12), 2133–51.

Choi, J. (2012). *Votes, Party Systems and Democracy in Asia*, London: Routledge.

Chua, C. (2008). *Chinese Big Business in Indonesia: The State of Capital*, London: Routledge.

Colombijn, F. (2018). The Production of Urban Space by Violence and its Aftermath in Jakarta and Kota Ambon, Indonesia. *Ethnos*, 83(1), 58–79.

Coppel, C. A. (1983). *Indonesian Chinese in Crisis*, Oxford University Press.

Coxhead, I & Li, M. (2008). Prospects for Skills-Based Export Growth in a Labour-Abundant, Resource-Rich Developing Country. *BIES*, 44(2), 209–38.

Cribb, R. & Coppel, C. A. (2009). A Genocide that Never Was: Explaining the Myth of Anti-Chinese Massacres in Indonesia, 1965–1966. *Journal of Genocide Research*, 11(4), 447–65.

Crouch, H. (2010). *Political Reform in Indonesia After Soeharto*, Singapore: ISEAS.

Crouch, M. (2014). *Law and Religion in Indonesia: Conflict and the Courts in West Java*, London: Routledge.

Davidson, J. S. (2007). Culture and Rights in Ethnic Violence. In J. S. Davidson & D. Henley, eds. *The Revival of Tradition in Indonesian Politics: The Deployment of Adat from Colonialism to Indigenism.* London: Routledge, pp. 224–46.

(2008). *From Rebellion to Riots: Collective Violence on Indonesian Borneo*, Madison: University of Wisconsin Press.

(2009). Dilemmas of Democratic Consolidation in Indonesia. *The Pacific Review*, 22(3), 293–310.

(2015a). *Indonesia's Changing Political Economy: Governing the Roads*, Cambridge University Press.

(2015b). The Demise of Indonesia's Upstream Oil and Gas Regulatory Agency: An Alternative Perspective. *Contemporary Southeast Asia*, 37 (1), 109–33.

(2016). Indonesia's New Governance Institutions: Accounting for their Varied Performance. *Asian Survey*, 56 (4), 651–75.

(2018). Then and Now: Campaigns to Achieve Rice Self-Sufficiency in Indonesia, *BKI*, 174(2–3), 188–215.

(n.d.) Profits and Property Rights: The Political Economy of Tollway Development in Indonesia, National University of Singapore, draft article.

Drexler, E. F. (2008). *Aceh, Indonesia: Securing the Insecure State*, Philadelphia: Pennsylvania University Press.

Duncan, C. R. (2013). *Violence and Vengeance: Religious Conflict and its Aftermath in Eastern Indonesia*, Ithaca: Cornell University Press.

Effendy, B. (2003). *Islam and the State in Indonesia*, Singapore: ISEAS.

Erb, M. (2016). Mining and the Conflict over Values in Nusa Tenggara Timur Province, Eastern Indonesia. *The Extractive Industries and Society*, 3(2), 370–82.

Erb, M. & Sulistiyanto, P., eds., (2009). *Deepening Democracy in Indonesia? Direct Elections for Local Leaders (Pilkada)*. Singapore: ISEAS.

Estrade, B. (1998). Fragmenting Indonesia: A Nation's Survival in Doubt. *World Policy Journal*, *XV*(3), 78–84.

Fay, C. & Denduangrudee, H. M. S. (2016). Emerging options for the recognition of protection of indigenous community rights in Indonesia. In J. F. McCarthy & K. Robinson, eds., *Land and Development in Indonesia: Searching for the People's Sovereignty*. Singapore: ISEAS, pp. 91–112.

Fealy, G. (2015). The Politics of Yudhoyono: Majoritarian Democracy, Insecurity, and Vanity. In E. Aspinall, M. Mietzner, & D. Tomsa, eds., *The Yudhoyono Presidency: Indonesia's Decade of Stability and Stagnation*. Singapore: ISEAS, pp. 35–54.

(2016a). Bigger than Ahok: Explaining the 2 December Mass Rally, December 7, Melbourne: Indonesia at Melbourne, http://indonesiaatmel bourne.unimelb.edu.au/bigger-than-ahok-explaining-jakartas-2-decem ber-mass-rally/.

(2016b). The Politics of Religious Intolerance in Indonesia: Mainstream-ism Trumps Extremism? In T. Lindsey & H. Pausacker, eds., *Religion, Law and Intolerance in Indonesia*, New York: Routledge, pp. 115–31.

Feillard, A. & Madinier, R. (2010). *The End of Innocence? Indonesian Islam and the Temptation of Radicalism*, Honolulu: The University of Hawaii Press.

Fionna, U. (2013). *The Institutionalisation of Political Parties in Post-authoritarian Indonesia: From the Grass-roots Up*, Amsterdam University Press.

(2014). Indonesian Parties Struggle for Electability. In U. Fionna, ed. *Watching the Indonesian 2014 Elections*. Singapore: ISEAS, pp. 8–15.

Fitrani, F., Hofman, B., & Kaiser, K. (2005). Unity in Diversity? The Creation of New Local Government in a Decentralizing Indonesia. *BIES*, 41(1), 57–79.

Ford, M. & Pepinsky, T. B. (2013). Beyond Oligarchy: Critical Exchanges on Political Power and Materal Inequality in Indonesia. *Indonesia*, 96, 1–9.

eds. (2014). *Beyond Oligarchy: Wealth, Power, and Contemporary in Indonesian Politics*, Ithaca: CSEAPP.

Formichi, C. (2012). *Islam and the Making of the Nation: Kartosuwiryo and Political Islam in 20th Century Indonesia*, Leiden: KITLV Press.

Fossati, D. (2016). Beyond "Good Governance": The Multi-level Politics of Health Insurance for the Poor in Indonesia. *World Development*, 87, 291–306.

(2017). From Periphery to Centre: Local Government and the Emergence of Universal Health Care in Indonesia. *Contemporary Southeast Asia*, 39(1), 178–203.

Fox, C. (2018). Candidate-centric systems and the politicization of ethnicity: evidence from Indonesia. *Democratization*, 25, forthcoming.

Fukuoka, Y. (2012). Politics, Business and the State in Post-Soeharto Indonesia. *Contemporary Southeast Asia*, 34(1), 80–100.

Geertz, C. (1960). *The Religion of Java*, Glencoe: The Free Press.

Gellert, P.K. (2010). Rival Transnational Networks, Domestic Politics and Indonesian Timber. *Journal of Contemporary Asia*, 40(4), 539–67.

Goebel, Z. (2015). *Language and Superdiversity: Indonesians Knowledging at Home and Aboard*, Oxford University Press.

Habir, A. D. (2013). Resource Nationalism and Constitutional Jihad. *Southeast Asian Affairs*, 13, 121–34.

Hadiz, V. R. (2010). *Localising Power in Post-Authoritarian Indonesia: A Southeast Asia Perspective*, Stanford University Press.

(2016). *Islamic Populism in Indonesia and the Middle East*, Cambridge University Press.

Hadiz, V. R. & Robison, R. (2013). The Political Economy of Oligarchy and the Reorganization of Power in Indonesia. *Indonesia*, 96, 35–57.

Hamayotsu, K. (2011). The Political Rise of the Prosperous Justice Party in Post-Authoritarian Indonesia. *Asian Survey*, 51(5), 971–92.

Hamilton-Hart, N. (2006). Terrorism in Southeast Asia. *Pacific Review*, 18(3), 303–25.

Hamilton-Hart, N. & Palmer, B. (2017). Co-Investment and Clientelism as Informal Institutions: Beyond "Good Enough" Property Rights Protection. *Studies in Comparative International Development*, 52(4), 416–35.

Hamilton-Hart, N. & Schulze, G. G. (2016). Taxing Times in Indonesia: The Challenge of Restoring Competitiveness and the Search for Fiscal Space. *BIES*, 52(3), 265–95.

Hanson, S. E. (2017). The Evolution of Regimes: What Can Twenty-Five Years of Post-Soviet Change Teach Us? *Perspectives on Politics*, 15(2), 328–41.

Harish, S. P. & Toha, R. J. (n.d.). A New Typology of Electoral Violence: Insights from Indonesia. *Terrorism and Political Violence*, forthcoming.

Hassan, N. (2006). *Laskyar Jihad: Islam, Militancy and the Quest for Identity in Post-New Order Indonesia*, Ithaca: CSEAPP.

(2010). The Failure of the Wahhabi Campaign: Transnational Islam and the Salafi Madrasah in Post 9/11 Indonesia. *SEAR*, 18(4), 675–705.

(2013). *The Making of Public Islam: Piety, Democracy, and Youth in Indonesian Politics*. Yogyakarta: Universitas Islam Negeri Sunan Kalijaga.

Hedman, E. L. E., ed. (2008). *Conflict, Violence and Displacement in Indonesia*, Ithaca: CSEAPP.

Hefner, R. W. (2000). *Civil Islam: Muslims and Democratization in Indonesia*, Princeton University Press.

(2018). Introduction. Indonesia at the Crossroads: Imbroglios of Religion, State, and Society in an Asian Muslim Nation. In R. W. Hefner, ed. *Routledge Handbook of Contemporary Indonesia*. London: Routledge, pp. 1–54.

Henley, D. & Davidson, J. S. (2008). In the Name of *Adat*: Regional Perspectives on Reform, Tradition and Democracy in Indonesia. *Modern Asian Studies*, 42(4), 815–52.

Hicks, J. (2012). The Missing Link: Explaining the Political Mobilisation of Islam in Indonesia. *Journal of Contemporary Asia*, 42(1), 39–66.

Hill, H. (2000). *The Indonesian Economy*, 2nd edn, Cambridge University Press.

(2015). The Indonesian Economy during the Yudhoyono Decade. In E. Aspinall, M. Mietzner, & D. Tomsa, eds., *The Yudhoyono Presidency: Indonesia's Decade of Stability and Stagnation*. Singapore: ISEAS, pp. 281–302.

Honna, J. (2012). Inside the Democrat Party: Power, Politics, and Conflict in Indonesia's Presidential Party. *SEAR*, 20(4), 473–89.

Hoon, C. Y. (2008). *Chinese Identity in Post-Suharto Indonesia: Culture, Politics, and Media*, Brighton: Sussex Academic Press.

Horowitz, D. L. (2003). *A Deadly Ethnic Riot*, Berkeley: University of California Press.

(2013). *Constitutional Change and Democracy in Indonesia*, Cambridge University Press.

Human Rights Watch (2010). *Unkept Promise: Failure to End Military Business Activity in Indonesia*, New York: Human Rights Watch.

(2013). *In the Name of Religious: Violence Minorities*, New York: Human Rights Watch.

(2016). *"These Political Games Ruin Our Lives": Indonesia's LGBT Community under Threat*. New York: Human Rights Watch.

Huntington, S. (1991). *Democracy's Third Wave: Democratization in the Late Twentieth Century*, Norman: Oklahoma University Press.

Hurst, W. (2018). *Ruling before the Law: The Politics of Legal Regimes in China and Indonesia*, Cambridge University Press.

Hwang, J. C. (2010). When Parties Swing: Islamist Parties and Institutional Moderation in Malaysia and Indonesia. *SEAR*, 18(4): 635–74.

(2018). *Why Terrorists Quit: The Disengagement of Indonesian Jihadists*, Ithaca: Cornell University Press.

Institute for Economic and Social Research – Faculty of Economic, University of Indonesia (LPEM-FEUI) and Asia Foundation (2009). The Cost of Moving Goods: Transportation, Regulations and Charges in Indonesia, Jakarta: Asia Foundation, http://asiafoundation.org/2008/04/14/the-cost-of-moving-goods-road-transportation-regulation-and-charges-in-indonesia/.

Isra, S. (2014). *10 Tahun Bersama SBY: Catatan Refleksi Dua Periode Kepemimpinan*, Jakarta: Kompas.

Jayasuriya, K. (2005). *Reconstituting the Global Liberal Order: Legitimacy and Regulation*, London: Routledge.

Jones, S. (2013). Indonesian Government Approaches to Radical Islam Since 1998. In M. Knkler & A. Stepan, eds., *Democracy and Islam in Indonesia*. New York: Columbia University Press, pp.109–25.

Jones, T. (2013). *Culture, Power, and Authoritarianism in the Indonesian State: Cultural Policy across the Twentieth Century to the Reform Era*, Leiden: Brill.

Kammen, D. (2017). Polarizing Indonesia. Paper presented at the conference "Two decades after 1998 Reformasi: achievements and challenges." November 11. Graduate Research Institute of Policy Studies, Tokyo.

Kammen, D. & McGregor, K. eds. (2012). *Contours of Mass Violence in Indonesia: 1965–1968*. Singapore: NUS Press.

Kersten, C. (2015). *Islam in Indonesia: The Contest for Society, Ideas, and Values*, London: Hurst & Company.

Kim, K. (2018). Matchmaking: Establishment of State-owned Holding Companies in Indonesia. *Asia & The Pacific Policy Studies*, 5 (2), 313–30.

Kimura, E. (2012). *Political Change and Territoriality in Indonesia; Provincial Proliferation*, New York: Routledge.

King, D. Y. (2003). *Half-hearted Reform: Electoral Institutions and the Struggle for Democracy in Indonesia*, Westport: Praeger.

Kuddus, R. (2017). The Ghosts of 1965: Politics and Memory in Indonesia. *New Left Review*, 104, 45–92.

Kunicová, J. & Rose-Ackerman, S. (2005). Electoral Rules and Constitutional Structures as Constraints on Corruption. *British Journal of Political Science*, 35(4), 573–606.

Kurniawati, D. (2017). Jakarta Election seen as "Battle for Country's Soul." *Asiansentinel.com*, February 13, www.asiasentinel.com/politics/jakarta-election-seen-as-battle-for-countrys-soul.

Kwok, Y. (2016). LGBT Rights in Indonesia Are Coming Under "Unprecedented Attack." *Time.com*, August 11, http://time.com/4447819/indonesia-lgbt-rights-islam-muslim-gay-bi-transgender/.

Laffan, M. (2011). *The Makings of Indonesian Islam: Orientalism and the Narration of a Sufi Past*, Princeton University Press.

Lane, M. (2008). *Unfinished Nation: Indonesia Before and After Suharto*, London: Verso/ Talisman.

Lev, D. S. (1966). *The Transition to Guided Democracy in Indonesia, 1957–1959*. Ithaca: Modern Indonesia Project, Cornell University.

(2000). *Legal Evolution and Political Authority in Indonesia: Selected Essays*, Leiden: Martinus Nijhoff Publishers.

Lewis, B. (2014). Twelve years of fiscal decentralization: a balance sheet. In H. Hill, ed., *Regional Dynamics in a Decentralized Indonesia.* Singapore: ISEAS, pp. 135–55.

Li, T. M. (2000). Articulating Indigenous Identity in Indonesia: Resource Politics and the Tribal Slot. *Comparative Studies in Society and History,* 42(1), 149–79.

    (2001). Masyarakat Adat, Difference, and the Limits of Recognition in Indonesia's Forest Zone. *Modern Asian Studies,* 35(3), 645–76.

Liddle, R. W. (1996). The Islamic Turn in Indonesia. A Political Expansion. *Journal of Asian Studies,* 55, 613–34.

    (2013). Improving the Quality of Democracy in Indonesia. *Indonesia,* 96, 59–80.

Liddle, R. W. & Mujani, S. (2007). Leadership, Party and Religion: Explaining Voting Behavior in Indonesia. *Comparative Political Studies,* 40(7), 832–57.

Lim, M. (2017). Social Media, Algorithmic Enclaves, and the Rise of Tribal Nationalism in Indonesia. *Critical Asian Studies,* 49(3), 411–27.

Lindsey, T. & Pausacker, H., eds. (2016). *Religion, Law and Intolerance in Indonesia,* New York: Routledge.

Lont, H. & White, B. (2003). Critical Review of Crisis Studies, 1998–2002: Debates on Poverty, Employment and Solidarity in Indonesia. In H. Schulte Nordholt & G. Anan, eds. *Indonesia in Transition: Work in Progress.* Yogyakarta: Pustaka Pelajar, pp. 125–59.

Machmudi, Y. (2008). *Islamising Indonesia: The Rise of the Jemaah Tarbiyah and the Prosperous Justice Party (PKS),* Canberra: ANU ePress.

MacIntrye, A. (2000). Funny Money: Fiscal Policy, Rent-seeking and Economic Performance in Indonesia. In M. H. Khan & K. S. Jomo, eds., *Rents, Rent-seeking and Economic Development: Theory and Evidence in Asia.* Cambridge University Press, pp. 274–303.

Mackie, J. A. C. (1976). Anti-Chinese Outbreaks in Indonesia, 1959–68. In J. A. C. Mackie, ed., *The Chinese in Indonesia.* Honolulu: The University Press of Hawaii, pp. 77–138.

Malley, M. (1999). Regions: Centralization and Resistance. In D. Emmerson, ed., *Indonesia beyond Suharto: Polity, Economy, and Society.* Armonk: M. E. Sharpe, pp. 71–108.

Manning, C. & Roesad, K. (2007). The Manpower Law of 2003 and its Implementing Regulations: Genesis, Key Articles and Potential Impact. *BIES,* 43(1), 59–86.

McBeth, J. (2016). *The Loner: President Yudhoyono's Decade of Trial and Indecision,* Singapore: Straits Times Press.

McCarthy, J. F. (2002). Turning in Circles: District Governance, Illegal Logging and Environmental Decline in Sumatra, Indonesia. *Society and Natural Resources*, 15: 867–86.

(2004). Changing to Gray: Decentralization and the Emergence of Volatile Socio-Legal Configurations in Central Kalimantan, Indonesia. *World Development*, 32(7), 1199–223.

McCulloch, N. (2008). Rice Prices and Poverty in Indonesia. *BIES*, 44(1), 45–64.

McLeod, R. H. (2005). The Struggle to Regain Effective Government under Democracy in Indonesia. *BIES*, 41(3), 367–86.

McRae, D. (2013). *A Few Poorly Organized Men: Interreligious Violence in Poso, Indonesia*, Leiden: Brill.

Melvin, J. (2018). *The Army and the Indonesian Genocide: Mechanics of Mass Murder*, London: Routledge.

Menchik, J. (2014). Productive Intolerance: Godly Nationalism in Indonesia. *Comparative Studies in Society and History*, 56(3), 591–621.

(2016). *Islam and Democracy in Indonesia: Tolerance without Liberalism*, Cambridge University Press.

Mietzner, M. (2010). Political Conflict Resolution and Democratic Consolidation in Indonesia: The Role of the Constitutional Court. *Journal of East Asian Studies*, 10(3), 397–424.

(2012). Indonesia's Democratic Stagnation: Anti-reformist Elites and Resilient Civil Society. *Democratization*, 19(2), 209–29.

(2013). *Money, Power, and Ideology: Political Parties in Post-Authoritarian Indonesia*, Singapore: NUS Press.

(2014a). Indonesia's Decentralization: The Rise of Local Identities and the Survival of the Nation-state. In H. Hill, ed., *Regional Dynamics in a Decentralized Indonesia*. Singapore: ISEAS, pp. 45–67.

(2014b). How Jokowi Won and Democracy Survived. *Journal of Democracy*, 25 (4), 111–25.

(2016). Coercing Loyalty: Coalitional Presidentialism and Party Politics in Jokowi's Indonesia. *Contemporary Southeast Asia*, 38(2), 209–32.

Miller, M. A. (2009). *Rebellion and Reform in Indonesia: Jakarta's Security and Autonomy Policies in Aceh*, New York: Routledge.

Millie, J. & Hindasah, L. (2015). Regional Aspects of the Indonesian Ulama Council's Ideological Turn. *Asia Pacific Journal of Anthropology*, 16(3), 260–81.

Negara, S. D. (2016). Indonesia's 2016 Budget: Optimism Amidst Global Uncertainties. *ISEAS Perspective*, 3, www.iseas.edu.sg/articles-commentaries/iseas-perspective/iseas-perspective-2016?limit=10&start=60.

Nolan, C., Jones, S. & Solahudin. (2014). The Political Impact of Carving Up Papua. In H. Hill, ed., *Regional Dynamics in a Decentralized Indonesia.* Singapore: ISEAS, pp. 409–32.

North, D. C. (1990). *Institutions, Institutional Change, and Economic Performance*, Cambridge University Press.

Oetomo, D. (1996). Gender and Sexual Orientation in Indonesia. In L. Sears, ed., *Fantasizing the Feminine.* Durham: Duke University Press, pp. 259–69.

Oetomo, D. & Sciortino, R. (2017). The LGBT Community: Youngest Stepchild? *The Jakarta* Post, January 11, www.thejakartapost.com/acade mia/2017/01/11/the-lgbt-community-youngest-stepchild.html.

Olken, B. A. (2006). Corruption and the Costs of Redistribution: Micro Evidence from Indonesia. *Journal of Public Economics*, 90, 853–80.

Oppenheimer, J. (2012).*The Act of Killing* (Austin: Drafthouse Films).
    (2014).*The Look of Silence* (Austin: Drafthouse Films).

Papanek, G. F., Pardede, R., & Nazara, S. (2014). *Economic Choices Facing the Next President*, Jakarta: Center for Public Policy Transformation.

Park, J. H. (n.d.). Rethinking Moderation: Electoral Performance of the Prosperous Justice Party in Indonesia. National University of Singapore, draft article.

Patunru, A. & Rahardja, S. (2015). Trade Protectionism in Indonesia: Bad Times and Bad Policy, July. Sydney: Lowy Institute for International Policy, www.lowyinstitute.org/publications/trade-protectionism-indonesia-bad-times-and-bad-policy.

Patunru, A. & Respatiadi H. (2017). Protecting the Farmers: Improving the Quality of Social Protection Schemes for Agricultural Workers in Indonesia. Jakarta: Center for Indonesian Policy Studies, www.cips-indonesia.org.

Peluso, N. (2018). Entangled Territories in Small-Scale Gold Mining Frontiers: Labor Practices, Property, and Secrets in Indonesian Gold Country. *World Development*, 101, 400–16.

Pepinsky, T. B. (2013). Pluralism and Political Conflict in Indonesia. *Indonesia*, 96, 81–100.

Pepinsky, T. B. & Wihardja, M. M. (2011). Decentralization and Economic Performance in Indonesia. *Journal of East Asian Studies*, 11(3), 337–71.

Pierskalla J. H. (2016). Splitting the Difference? The Politics of District Creation in Indonesia. *Comparative Politics*, 48(2), 249–68.

Pierskalla, J. H. and Sacks, A. (2017). Unpacking the Effect of Decentralized Governance on Routine Violence: Lessons from Indonesia. *World Development*, 90, 213–28.

Pisani, E., Kok, M. O., & Nugroho, K. (2017) Indonesia's Road to Universal Health Coverage. *Health Policy and Planning*, 32(2), 267–76.

Platzdasch, B. (2013). Religious Freedom in Contemporary Indonesia: The Case of Ahmadiyah. In Y. F. Hui, ed., *Encountering Islam: The Politics of Religious Identities in Southeast Asia*. Singapore: ISEAS, pp. 218–46.

Pompe, S. (2005). *The Indonesian Supreme Court: A Study of Institutional Collapse*, Ithaca: CSEAPP.

Posner, R. (1998). Creating a Legal Framework for Economic Development. *The World Bank Research Observer*, 13(1), 1–11.

Purdey, J. (2006). *Anti-Chinese Violence in Indonesia, 1996–1999*, Singapore: NUS Press.

   (2016). Narratives to Power: The Case of the Djojohadikusmo Family Dynasty over Generations. *SEAR*, 24(3), 369–85.

Purnomo, H. Shantiko, B., Sitorus, S., et al. (2017). Fire Economy and Actor Network of Forest and Land Fires in Indonesia. *Forest Policy and Economics*, 78, 21–31.

Qodari, M. (2010). The Professionalisation of Politics: The Growing Role of Polling Organisations and Political Consultants. In E. Aspinall & M. Mietzner, eds., *Problems of Democratisation in Indonesia: Elections, Institutions, and Society*. Singapore: ISEAS, pp. 122–40.

Rachman, N. F. (2017). *Petani and Penguasa: Dinamika Perjalanan Politik Agraria Indonesia*, 2nd edn, Yogyakarta: Insist Press.

Reid, A., ed. (2006). *Verandah of Violence: The Background to the Aceh Problem*. Singapore University Press.

Reilly, B. (2006). *Democracy and Diversity: Political Engineering in the Asia Pacific*, Oxford University Press.

Rhode, D. (2001). Indonesia Unraveling? *Foreign Affairs*, 80(4), 110–24.

Ricklefs, M. C. (2012). *Islamisation and Its Opponents in Java, c. 1930 to the Present*, Singapore: NUS Press.

Rigg, J. (2016). *Challenging Southeast Asian Development: The Shadows of Success*, London: Routledge.

Robinson, G. B. (2009). *"If You Leave Us Here, We Will Die": How Genocide Was Stopped in East Timor*, Princeton University Press.

   (2018). *The Killing Season: A History of the Indonesian Massacres, 1965–66*, Princeton University Press.

Robison, R. (1986). *Indonesia: The Rise of Capital*, Sydney: Allen & Unwin/ Asian Studies Association of Australia.

Robison, R. & Hadiz, V. R. (2004). *Reorganising Power in Indonesia: The Politics of Oligarchy in an Age of Markets*, London: RoutledgeCurzon.

Rock, M. T. (2017). *Dictators, Democrats, and Development in Southeast Asia: Implications for the Rest*, Oxford University Press.

Roosa, J. (2006). *Pretext for Mass Murder: The September 30th Movement and Suharto's Coup d'État in Indonesia*, Madison: University of Wisconsin Press.

Rosser, A. (2002). *The Politics of Economic Liberalisation in Indonesia: State, Market and Power, Richmond*, Surrey: Curzon.

  (2012). Realising Free Health Care for the Poor in Indonesia: The Politics of Illegal Fees. *Journal of Contemporary Asia*, 42 (2), 255–75.

Rudnyckyj, D. (2010). *Spiritual Economies: Islam, Globalization, and the Afterlife of Development*, Ithaca: Cornell University Press.

Rutherford, D. & Mote, O. (2001). From Irian Jaya to *Papua*: The Limits of Primordialism in Indonesia's Troubled East. *Indonesia*, 72, 115–40.

Saich, A., Pincus, J., Dapice, D., et al. (2010). From Reformasi to Institutional Transformation: A Strategic Assessment of Indonesia's Prospects for Growth, Equity and Democratic Governance. Cambridge, MA: Ash Center for Democratic Governance and Innovation, Harvard Kennedy School, https://ash.harvard.edu/links/reformasi-institutional-transformation-strategic-assessment-indonesias-prospects-growth.

Salim, A. (2008). The Shari'a Bylaws and Human Rights in Indonesia. *Studia Islamika*, 15(1), 1–23.

Sato, Y. (2005). Bank Restructuring and Financial Institution Reform in Indonesia. *The Developing Economies*, *XLIII* (1), 91–120.

Sawit, M. H. & Lokollo, E. M. (2007). *Rice Import Surge in Indonesia*. Bogor: The Indonesian Center for Agriculture Socio-Economic and Policy Studies, in collaboration with The ActionAid International.

Schulte Nordholt, H. (2003) Renegotiating Boundaries: Access, Agency and Identity in Post-Soeharto Indonesia. *BKI*, 159(4), 550–89.

Schütte, S. A. (2017). Two Steps Forward, One Step Backwards: Indonesia's Winding (Anti-)Corruption Journey. In T. Gong & I. Scott, eds., *Routledge Handbook of Corruption in Asia*. London: Routledge, pp. 42–55.

Sherlock, S. (2010). The Parliament in Indonesia's Decade of Democracy: People's Forum or Chamber of Cronies? In E. Aspinall & M. Mietzner, eds. *Problems of Democratization in Indonesia: Elections, Institutions and Society.* Singapore: ISEAS, pp. 160–78.

Shiraishi, T. 1990. *Age in Motion: Popular Radicalism in Java, 1912–1926*, Ithaca: Cornell University Press.

Sidel, J. (2006). *Riots, Pogroms, Jihad: Religious Violence in Indonesia*, Ithaca: Cornell University Press.

Slater, D. (2004). Indonesia's Accountability Trap: Party Cartels and Presidential Power after Democratic Transition. *Indonesia*, 78, 61–92.

Smith, B. (2008). The Origins of Regional Autonomy in Indonesia: Experts and the Making of Political Interests. *Journal of East Asian Studies*, 8(2), 211–34.

Suryadinata, L. (2001). Chinese Politics in Post-Suharto's Indonesia: Beyond the Ethnic Approach? *Asian Survey*, 41(3), 502–24.

Syailendra, E. A. (2017). In the Name of Food Security. *Inside Indonesia*, 127, January–March, www.insideindonesia.org/in-the-name-of-food-security.

Tadjoeddin, M. Z. (2014). *Explaining Collective Violence in Contemporary Indonesia: From Conflict to Cooperation*, Basingstoke: Palgrave MacMillan.

Tan, P. J. (2015). Explaining Party System Institutionalization in Indonesia. In A. Hicken & E. M. Kuhonta, eds., *Party System Institutionalization in Asia: Democracies, Autocracies, and the Shadows of the Past*. Cambridge University Press, pp. 236–59.

Tans, R. (2012). *Mobilizing Resources, Building Coalitions: Local Power in in Indonesia*, East-West Center Policy Studies, No. 64, Honolulu.

Tanter, R., Ball, D., & van Klinken, G., eds. (2006). *Masters of Terror: Indonesia's Military and Violence in East Timor*. Lanham: Rowman & Littlefield Publishers.

Tanuwidjaja, S. (2010). Political Islam and Islamic Parties in Indonesia: Critically Assessing the Evidence of Islam's Political Decline. *Contemporary Southeast Asia*, 32(1), 29–49.

(2012). PKS in Post-Reformasi Indonesia: Catching the Catch-All and Moderation Wave. *SEAR*, 20(4), 533–49.

Tapsell, R. (2015). Indonesia's Media Oligarchy and the "Jokowi Phenomenon." *Indonesia*, 99, 38–48.

Toha, R. J. (2017). Political Competition and Ethnic Riots in Democratic Transition: A Lesson from Indonesia. *British Journal of Political Science*, 47(3), 631–51.

Tomsa, D. (2010). Indonesian Politics in 2010: Perils of Stagnation. *BIES*, 46(3), 309–28.

(2012). Moderating Islamism in Indonesia: Tracing Patterns of Party Change in the Prosperous Justice Party. *Political Research Quarterly*, 65(3), 486–98.

(2014). Party System Fragmentation in Indonesia: The Subnational Dimension. *Journal of East Asian Studies*, 14(2), 249–78.

(2015). Toning Down the "Big Bang": The Politics of Decentralization During the Yudhoyono Years. In E. Aspinall, M. Mietzner, & D. Tomsa, eds. *The Yudhoyono Presidency: Indonesia's Decade of Stability and Stagnation*, Singapore: ISEAS, pp. 155–74.

Ufen, A. (2008). Political Party and Party System Institutionalization in Southeast Asia: Lessons for Democratic Consolidation in Indonesia, the Philippines, and Thailand. *The Pacific Review*, 21(3), 327–50.

van Bruinessen, M. (2002). Genealogies of Islamic Radicalism in post-Suharto Indonesia. *SEAR*, 10(2), 117–54.

(2013a). Overview of Muslim Organizations, Associations and Movements in Indonesia. In M. van Bruinessen, ed., *Contemporary Developments in Indonesian Islam: Explaining the "Conservative Turn."* Singapore: ISEAS, pp. 21–58.

(2013b). Introduction: Contemporary Developments in Indonesian Islam: Explaining the "Conservative Turn." In M. van Bruinessen, ed., *Contemporary Developments in Indonesian Islam: Explaining the "Conservative Turn."* Singapore: ISEAS, pp.1–20.

van Klinken, G. (2007). *Communal Violence and Democratization in Indonesia: Small Town Wars*, London: Routledge.

van Klinken, G. & Barker, J., eds. (2009). *State of Authority: The State in Society in Indonesia*, Ithaca: CSEAPP.

Varkkey, H. (2016). *The Haze Problem in Southeast Asia: Palm Oil and Patronage*, Routledge: New York.

Varshney, A., Tadjoeddin, M. Z, & Panggabean, R. (2008). Creating Datasets in Information-Poor Environments: Patterns of Collective Violence in Indonesia, 1990–2003. *Journal of East Asian Studies*, 8(3), 361–94.

von Luebke, C. (2009). The Political Economy of Local Governance: Findings from an Indonesian Field Study. *BIES*, 45(2), 201–30.

Warburton, E. (2016). Jokowi and the New Developmentalism. *BIES*, 52(3), 297–320.

Warr, P. (2011). Poverty, Food Prices and Economic Growth in Southeast Asian Perspective. In C. Manning & S. Sumarto, eds. *Employment, Living Standards and Poverty in Contemporary Indonesia*. Singapore: ISEAS, pp. 47–67.

Webber, D. (2006). A Consolidated Patrimonial Democracy? Democratization in Indonesia. *Democratization*, 13(3), 396–420.

Wilson, C. (2011). *Ethno-Religious Violence in Indonesia: From Soil to God*, London: Routledge.

Wilson, I. (2015). *The Politics of Protection Rackets in Post-New Order Indonesia: Coercive Capital, Authority and Street Politics*, London: Routledge.

Winters, J. (2011). *Oligarchy*, Cambridge University Press.

(2013). Oligarchy and Democracy in Indonesia. *Indonesia*, 96, 11–33.

World Bank. (2004). *Indonesia: Averting an Infrastructure Crisis: A Framework for Policy and Action*, Washington, DC: The World Bank, http://documents.worldbank.org/curated/en/418771468771672348/Indonesia-Averting-an-infrastructure-crisis-a-framework-for-policy-and-action.

(2005). *Raising Investment in Indonesia: A Second Generation of Reforms*, Report No. 31708-ID, Washington, DC: The World Bank, http://documents.worldbank.org/curated/en/813951468752955838/Raising-investments-in-Indonesia-a-second-generation-of-reforms.

(2016). *Indonesia's Rising Divide*, Washington, DC: The World Bank, http://documents.worldbank.org/curated/en/267671467991932516/Indonesias-rising-divide.

Ziegenhain, P. (2008). *The Indonesian Parliament and Democratization*, Singapore: ISEAS.

# Acknowledgments

I would like to express my deep appreciation to the series editors, Ed Aspinall and Meredith Weiss, for inviting to write this book. I also thank Shane Barker, Gustav Brown, Ulla Fionna, Diego Fossati, Kikue Hamayotsu, Hui Yew-Foong, Terence Lee, George May, Erik Mobrand, Deepk Nair, William Nessen, Dirk Tomsa, and Ericssen Wen for offering constructive advice on parts of the manuscript. The lovely and brainy Portia Reyes, Ed Aspinall, and three anonymous reviewers graciously read the whole book, laying the path for revisions with clear guideposts. Conversations with Douglas Kammen also kept the revision process on the right track. I dedicate this book to that youthful generation that despised dictatorship and that made Iwan Fals a legend. May there be many more to come.

Cambridge Elements ≡

# Politics and Society in Southeast Asia

## Edward Aspinall

*Australian National University*

Edward Aspinall is a professor of politics at the Coral Bell School
of Asia-Pacific Affairs, Australian National University. A specialist of Southeast
Asia, especially Indonesia, much of his research has focused on democratisation,
ethnic politics and civil society in Indonesia and, most recently, clientelism
across Southeast Asia.

## Meredith L. Weiss

*University at Albany, SUNY*

Meredith L. Weiss is Professor of Political Science at the University at Albany,
SUNY. Her research addresses political mobilization and contention,
the politics of identity and development, and electoral politics in Southeast Asia.
She is active in the American Political Science Association and Association
for Asian Studies and has held visiting fellowships or professorships
at universities in the US, Malaysia, Singapore, the Philippines,
Japan, and Australia.

## About the Series

The Elements series Politics and Society in Southeast Asia includes
both country-specific and thematic studies on one of the world's most dynamic
regions. Each title, written by a leading scholar of that country or theme,
combines a succinct, comprehensive, up-to-date overview of debates
in the scholarly literature with original analysis and a clear argument.

Cambridge Elements ☰

# Politics and Society in Southeast Asia

Elements in the Series

A full series listing is available at: www.cambridge.org/ESEA